Jackie's Treasures

Jackie's Treasures

The Fabled Objects from the Auction of the Century

Dianne Russell Condon

Foreword by
Dominick Dunne

CADER BOOKS

CLARKSON POTTER/PUBLISHERS
NEW YORK

For Clifford and Owen,
my greatest treasures

ACKNOWLEDGMENTS

My many thanks are extended to the following people:

To Dona Chernoff, for pointing me in the right direction; to Kim Witherspoon, for her confidence in the project and her perseverance; to Chip Gibson, for recognizing a good thing; to Rick Maiman, for sharing an exciting morning and getting some great pictures in the process; to Roy Finamore, for keeping me focused; to Okie Slattery, for helping find the magic; to Stevie, for picking up the slack; to Alan Goodrich at the Kennedy Library, for sharing his wealth of knowledge; and to Michael Cader, for his wisdom, calm patience and sound guidance.

Much love and gratitude is also due to Cliff, for listening without interfering and to Christine, for loving my son. And to all my other friends and family whose words of support and enthusiasm kept me excited—thank you.

Text copyright © 1996 by Dianne Russell Condon
Foreword © 1996 by Dominick Dunne. This article originally appeared in *Vanity Fair*. Reprinted by permission of the William Morris Agency, Inc., on behalf of the author.

PHOTO CREDITS: Pages 2, 13, 15, 17, 18, 20, 21, 23, 24, 26 and 27, 28 (far left), 29, 31, 33, 35, 37, 39, 43 (left), 44 and 45, 47, 48, 50, 54, 55 (upper right), 56, 57, 58, 59, 62, 63, 84, and 85 courtesy of The John F. Kennedy Library. Pages 6, 10, 11, 12, 14, 19, 22, 25, 27 (inset), 28 (near left), 30, 31, 32, 36, 38, 41 (center; upper and lower right), 42, 43, 44, 45, 46 (left), 49, 51, 53, 58, 60, 61, 63, 65, 66, 67, 68 and 69, 69, 73, 74, 75, 76, 77, 78, 79, 80, 81, 82, 96, and 97 courtesy of Rick Maiman/Sygma. Pages 64, 71, 73, and 75 (upper right) courtesy of Archive.

Published by Clarkson Potter/Publishers, 201 East 50th Street, New York, New York 10022. Member of the Crown Publishing Group.

Random House, Inc. New York, Toronto, London, Sydney, Auckland

http://www.randomhouse.com/

Clarkson N. Potter, Potter, and colophon are trademarks of Clarkson N. Potter, Inc.

Printed in the United States of America

Design by Charles Kreloff and Jessica Shatan

Produced by Cader Books, 38 East 29th Street, New York, New York 10016

Library of Congress Cataloging-in-Publication Data

Condon, Dianne Russell.
    Jackie's treasures : the fabled objects from the auction of the century / Dianne Russell Condon. — 1st ed.
        p.   cm.
    1. Onassis, Jacqueline Kennedy, 1929–   —Estate—Catalogs.
    2. Art—Catalogs.   I. Title.
    N5220.05C68 1996
    707'.4—Ju28
9629242
CIP

ISBN 0–517–70832–9
10 9 8 7 6 5 4 3 2 1
First Edition

Contents

JACKIE'S JEWELRY ∾ 52

ARTS AND LEISURE ∾ 72

Foreword

Of course, she always seemed remote, aloof, private in the extreme, and unattainable, yet people, even people who had never met her, called her Jackie when they talked about her, because she was a part of the personal history of every American who was alive on that terrible day thirty years ago, recalled each time someone asks, "Do you remember where you were on the day President Kennedy was shot?" That day her image became engraved on our souls. If she enjoyed privilege, her privilege was never resented, because she had earned it with her courage. In New York, she could be seen doing the things that all New Yorkers do—hailing cabs, going to work, walking in Central Park, taking in a movie on Lexington Avenue. Apart from the pesky paparazzi, people did not intrude on her privacy, except maybe to call out, "Hi, Jackie" when they passed her, and some of them received a smile back, or a wave, as she kept on walking her fast walk, with her eyes raised just high enough to avoid eye contact, in the celebrity manner of seeing by not seeing called blindsight. Once, I saw her standing on a long line for the ladies' room at Radio City Music Hall during an intermission at Francis Ford Coppola's reissue of Abel Gance's great film, *Napoleon*. I can think of a whole list of people far less famous than she who would have found a way to get to the head of that line.

The public easily tires of icons, but America's fascination with Jacqueline Bouvier Kennedy Onassis never burned out; it remained as constant as the eternal flame she designated for her husband's grave. Her fame was free of the resentment that fame sometimes produces, because she didn't work at it, and she never grabbed for the perks that accompany it. No publicists plotted her course. Nor perfume company paid for her name to advertise its product. She was simply who she was, part of the fabric of American culture. In grand circles, the word "class" is considered a bad-taste word, but class is really the key word to describe her. Style, chic, and other such attributes are acquirable; class is not. Either you have it or you don't. Jackie had it in spades.

—DOMINICK DUNNE

A Lasting Look

THE LOOK THAT DEFINED A GENERATION.

In the end there was magic. It was a magic we were all familiar with, a magic we were ready quickly to embrace again—if only for a few short days. The auction of Jacqueline Kennedy Onassis's estate afforded us more than a rare glimpse of her private world; it gave us the chance to feel the magic of Camelot once again and pay homage to its queen. Jacqueline Kennedy was as close to royalty as this country will ever know. She might have preferred to be called "Jack-leen," but she was simply Jackie to the world that adored her.

In 1960 the Kennedys ushered into the White House a new era, an era of youth, vitality, and hope. With that, Jackie brought glamour and class.

Jackie set the standard by which we judge the modern First Lady. She was much more than a gracious hostess; she was a historian, giving the White House its rightful role as America's historic home; an ambassador charming heads of state around the world with her fluency of language and deep knowledge of world history; a champion of culture, making the arts and humanities a greater part of American life by welcoming leading musicians, dancers, and writers to the White House; a model wife; and a devoted mother. Ultimately, Jackie was America's national treasure.

She taught us about elegance, shimmering as she entered a room; about charm, possessing the ability to put a prince or a pauper at ease; and of course about dignity, carrying the grief of a nation with her on that saddest weekend in November 1963.

Jackie was a rare woman. She remained a public figure most of her life, yet masterfully retained her privacy. She was the most recognizable woman in the world, yet she seldom made public appearances and infrequently sat for interviews. In the past thirty years, those not personally acquainted with her had rarely heard her speak.

All this contributed to the aura surrounding the Sotheby's auction. For the first time, we could see some of the possessions that Jackie had acquired in her lifetime, things that she had lived with and loved.

The orchestration of the event anticipated every last detail. Work began nearly two years before, shortly after Jackie's death, when Sotheby's was contacted by her family to discuss the logistics of an auction. Over 5,000 items were included in the sale.

AUCTION–GOERS LINING UP IN FRONT OF SOTHEBY'S, NEW YORK.

Sotheby's meticulously went through the collection, cataloging each piece and estimating its value. The objects ran the gamut from historic antiques to lavish jewels to everyday trinkets, although the family chose not to include many personal items, such as clothing, sunglasses, and scarves, feeling that such objects would detract from the model of dignity and propriety that Jackie always represented.

The sale catalog, a comprehensive chronicle of the items to be auctioned, sold nearly 100,000 copies, and its purchase became the means by which tickets to a public exhibition were awarded.

The week-long event started at 8:00 A.M. on April 19, 1996, with the press preview, which attracted correspondents from forty countries as well as overwhelming numbers of American magazine, TV show, and news organization personnel. The general public was allowed in several hours later. For many of these people, the trip to Sotheby's was more a pilgrimage than a preview. Sotheby's felt privileged to host such a historic auction and their employees worked feverishly through the night readying the exhibition halls for the opening.

The result was spectacular. As the doors to 1334 York Avenue opened, the magic unfolded before the viewer's eyes. Welcoming the public atop the grand staircase was a larger-than-life image of a young, radiant Jackie, casually clad in jodhpurs. Photographic blowups of Jackie, serious and smiling, casual and elegant, served as a constant reminder throughout the exhibition of her personal connection to the objects filling the rooms. Many spectators had a glazed look of wonder in their eyes.

DIANE BROOKS, PRESIDENT AND CEO, SOTHEBY'S, NEW YORK.

ENTHUSIASTIC BIDDERS ON OPENING NIGHT.

The exhibition was scrupulously organized to reflect different aspects of Jackie's life. "Rooms" were created to display furniture, evoking Jackie's own apartment and the ambience that she created. Old masters graced the walls above overstuffed sofas, porcelain vases and candelabras sat atop antique tables. Around a corner, in the large center room, the eye was immediately drawn to a grouping of the president's possessions, his golf clubs casually leaning by his rocker with a portrait of Jackie looking down on them.

A third room held Jackie's jewelry, luxurious and simple, laid out in row after row of well-lit cases.

Toward the end of the viewing, more than one dazed admirer might wonder: Where did she keep all of this? Some of the objects came from her homes in Bernardsville, New Jersey's horse country, and Martha's Vineyard, but most were from her Manhattan apartment.

Jackie's Fifth Avenue apartment was luxurious, certainly, but in a low-key, comfortable way, not like a designer showplace. She filled her home with mementos of her life. Jackie wasn't the type to re-decorate every few years; if she liked something or if it had sentimental value, she kept it for years.

Over the years Jackie had lived in many places; her townhouse in Georgetown; the White House; the Harriman home in Washington, D.C., graciously lent to Jackie when she had to abruptly leave the White House, Aristotle's house on Scorpios; her New York apartment. With each move, she carefully selected the things that were important to her and brought them along, making each place home.

It was the lure of these treasures that drew un-precedented numbers of people to Sotheby's. Jackie's belongings brought her to life again and made people wonder—when filling a vase with flowers, did she reflect on her days as a young sena-tor's wife, when that same vase sat on her George-town mantel? When she sat down at her desk to write a note, did the magnitude of where she was sitting hit her? Every so often did she thumb through *Profiles in Courage*, just because?

That's what treasured pieces do—allow you to live with them in the present, while always provid-ing a window to the past. That's why we all collect and keep things, and Jackie was no different.

As Jackie's treasures go out into the world, her spirit will go with them. To all who admired her, that's a comforting thought.

SOTHEBY'S SET UP A SPECIAL AUCTION HOTLINE TO HANDLE THE UNPRECEDENTED AMOUNT OF PHONE CALLS. ONE-FIFTH OF ALL THE CALLS WERE ABOUT THIS BLACK AND GOLD ENAMEL LIGHTER, ESTIMATED TO SELL FOR $300–400. THE FINAL PRICE WAS $85,000.

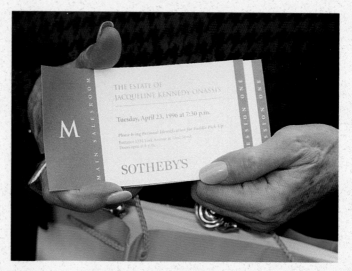

THE HOTTEST TICKET IN TOWN.

Jackie's Treasures

At Home in the White House

⊰⊱

As First Lady, Jackie strongly believed that her primary role was to make sure that the president's personal life was relaxed, fulfilling, and comfortable: "I want to take such good care of my husband that whatever he is doing, he can do better because he has me." Creating a beautiful home in the White House was an integral part of that job.

Making sure the White House met the needs of a young family with rambunctious children that was also the First Family was not easy, but Jackie managed it with her usual grace. She began by renovating the upstairs apartment that was the family's private quarters. "I want my children to be brought up in a personal environment, not in state rooms," she explained. One of her first projects was to transform a Truman-era guest room into a little girl's wonderland. An adjoining guest room became John's nursery. Under Jackie's guidance, the White House became a family home.

Jackie believed the public White House should be a house of the people and a reflection of the history of the presidency. Before the Kennedys moved in, the White House was a jumble of styles from previous administrations. Given a tour of her new home by Mamie Eisenhower, Jackie exclaimed that it looked as if it had been furnished from "a wholesale furniture store during a January clearance." Determined to make it an American showcase, she initiated a monumental restoration project that

THE WHITE HOUSE RED ROOM.

was quickly embraced by her husband. Working day and night with a curator, she combed the White House basement and storage rooms, trying to salvage many of the original furnishings. Jackie scrutinized every detail—fabric, wallpaper, and paint colors—making sure everything was just right. When the project was complete, the White House was a proud symbol of a renewed America and a stunning reflection of Jackie's deep sense of history and impeccable taste.

Jackie's White House Bedroom

Jackie's bedroom offered an oasis of tranquillity, tastefully furnished with many of her favorite possessions. No one knew what to expect on the first night of the auction; the prices fetched by the owl painting seen here and the famous mahogany footstool, two of the first items on the auction block, became a good indication of the wild bidding to come.

THIS STUDY OF A SNOW OWL (ABOVE, RIGHT) TRAVELED WITH JACKIE THROUGHOUT HER LIFE, PROMINENTLY HANGING ABOVE THE MANTEL IN HER BEDROOM IN THE WHITE HOUSE (FAR RIGHT). SHE LATER HUNG IT IN THE LIVING ROOM OF HER FIFTH AVENUE APARTMENT.

THE 12½-INCH-HIGH MAHOGANY FOOTSTOOL BEARS THE LABEL, "FOR CAROLINE TO CLIMB ONTO WINDOW SEAT."

SNOW OWL PICTURE
ESTIMATE: $2,000
PRICE: $31,050

~~~

FOOTSTOOL
ESTIMATE: $100-150
PRICE: $33,350

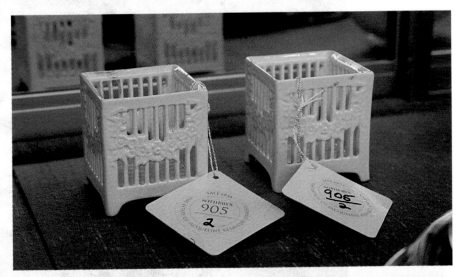

THE LOW ESTIMATES SOTHEBY'S
ORIGINALLY SET FOR EVERYDAY ITEMS
SUCH AS THESE SIMPLE EARTHENWARE
TUBS MADE THE GENERAL PUBLIC FEEL
THAT JACKIE'S POSSESSIONS WERE
ACCESSIBLE TO EVERYONE. ABSENTEE
BIDS FLOODED IN FROM THOUSANDS OF
FIRST-TIME SOTHEBY'S CLIENTS HOPING
TO MAKE JACKIE'S TREASURES THEIR
OWN. CLOSE TO 200 ITEMS WERE
ORIGINALLY VALUED AT UNDER $200;
ONLY FOUR ACTUALLY SOLD FOR LESS
THAN $2,000.

THE FIRST LADY'S BED AND DRESSING
TABLE.

EARTHENWARE TUBS
ESTIMATE: $60–90
PRICE: $6,325

⟶

CHAIRS
ESTIMATE: $1,500–2,000
PRICE: $25,300

PERFECTLY COMPLEMENTING THE
DECOR OF JACKIE'S WHITE HOUSE
BEDROOM, THIS PAIR OF NEOCLASSICAL
BLUE-AND-WHITE-PAINTED ARMCHAIRS
ORIGINALLY GRACED THE KENNEDYS'
GEORGETOWN RESIDENCE.

A Devoted Mother

Caroline and John were the center of Jackie's world. Active First Lady, enchanting stateswoman, stylish trendsetter, Jackie was first and foremost a mom. As First Lady, Jackie made sure that she had plenty of time each day to play with her children, and her adventurous spirit lent itself perfectly to motherhood. Weaving tales of magical characters and far-off lands, Jackie would enchant Caroline and John for hours. During summers in Hyannisport Jackie would play tirelessly on the beach, much like a child herself.

Jackie took advantage of her children's proximity to their father's office, often bringing them down to the Oval Office for a surprise visit, much to everyone's delight. Unfazed by their surroundings, John and Caroline would play at JFK's feet, and squeals of laughter would echo in the halls.

Jackie was fiercely protective of her children's privacy. She surrounded their White House playground with bushes to shield them from public scrutiny and kept them away from the press as much as possible. She accepted the fact that she and her husband were continually in the eye of an admiring public, who doted on their every move, but she drew the line at her children, carefully regulating their appearances in the media. Proud of her children's accomplishments, she remarked on several occasions that she felt her greatest feat was raising two relatively normal children under highly unusual circumstances. They are her legacy.

JACKIE INTRODUCES CAROLINE AND JOHN JR. TO THE JOYS OF NATURE.

PASSING ON A LIFELONG LOVE OF READING.

A Little Girl's Wonderland

Three-year-old Caroline adapted easily to her new home in the White House. Jackie set up a nursery school for her on the third floor, where she was often seen frolicking with her playmates and many pets. Caroline spent endless hours playing in her room, which her mother had lovingly decorated. With its pink walls and canopy bed, the room brought to life every little girl's fantasy.

ROCKING HORSE
ESTIMATE: $2,000–3,000
PRICE: $85,000

PERHAPS THE MOST FAMOUS ROCKING HORSE IN THE WORLD CAN BE SEEN HERE IN CAROLINE'S BEDROOM. DATING BACK TO THE EARLY 1900S, IT IS COVERED IN HIDE AND NEARLY FOUR FEET LONG.

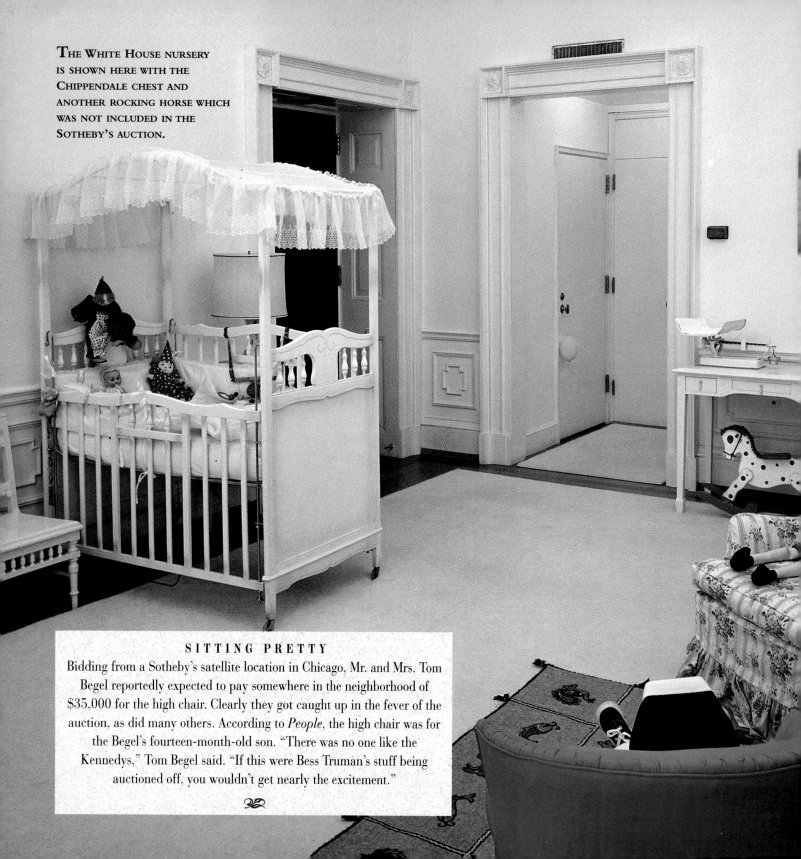

THE WHITE HOUSE NURSERY
IS SHOWN HERE WITH THE
CHIPPENDALE CHEST AND
ANOTHER ROCKING HORSE WHICH
WAS NOT INCLUDED IN THE
SOTHEBY'S AUCTION.

SITTING PRETTY
Bidding from a Sotheby's satellite location in Chicago, Mr. and Mrs. Tom Begel reportedly expected to pay somewhere in the neighborhood of $35,000 for the high chair. Clearly they got caught up in the fever of the auction, as did many others. According to *People*, the high chair was for the Begel's fourteen-month-old son. "There was no one like the Kennedys," Tom Begel said. "If this were Bess Truman's stuff being auctioned off, you wouldn't get nearly the excitement."

White House Nursery

Born after JFK was elected president, John Jr. symbolized the youth and vitality of the new administration. Not since Lincoln had the White House been home to such an energetic clan, and John Jr. grew up in the White House as no other child had, or has since. John Jr. and his father spent many happy hours playing in his White House bedroom. John Jr.'s childhood dresser was auctioned, as well as the mahogany high chair that he used in the White House.

THIS SIMPLE WHITE CHIPPENDALE CHEST OF DRAWERS WAS PERFECT FOR THE NEW BABY'S ROOM.

THE VICTORIAN HIGH CHAIR, MAHOGANY AND UPHOLSTERED IN VELVET, WAS USED BY JOHN JR. DURING HIS TODDLER YEARS IN THE WHITE HOUSE.

CHIPPENDALE CHEST
ESTIMATE: $600–800
PRICE: $13,800

HIGH CHAIR
ESTIMATE: $1,500–2,000
PRICE: $85,300

The West Sitting Room

Senators, ambassadors, and heads of state might come and go downstairs, but the family quarters were strictly private. Ever mindful of keeping the White House a home, Jackie designed this room tastefully and comfortably—encouraging its use as a true family room, complete with picture books and puzzles for the whole family to enjoy. This became the gathering place where the Kennedys would read and relax.

Jackie was a wonderful hostess even before it became her official role, and she often threw informal dinner parties in her Georgetown home. Conversation around the dining room table, where the cane-backed chairs seen here were originally placed, was always spirited.

SET OF SIX
LOUIS XVI-STYLE CHAIRS
ESTIMATE:
$2,500-3,500
PRICE:
$16,100

Jackie first arranged a set of six Louis
XVI-style cane-backed chairs around
the Kennedy's Georgetown dining room.
She later moved them to the White
House, where several were used in the
West Sitting Room (far left) along with
a complimentary pair of Louis XVI-style
chairs with arm rests (above).

Pair of Louis XVI-Style Chairs

Estimate:
$1,500–2,000
Price:
$8,050

Jackie's father, John "Black Jack" Bouvier, was known as a drinker, gambler, and womanizer, and his marriage to Jackie's mother ended in a bitter divorce. But through it all Jackie adored him, and he was an ever-indulgent father. She and her sister, Lee, spent many fun-filled weekends and summers with him, and throughout her life Jackie remained a devoted daughter.

The desk in the West Sitting Room, which Jackie often used, was one of the few items she owned that had belonged to her father, and its sentimental value was evident in the sale price.

EMPIRE-STYLE DESK
ESTIMATE: $1,500-2,000
PRICE: $68,500

LE HOFGARTEN À BAYREUTH
ESTIMATE: $800-1,200
PRICE: $33,500

JOHN BOUVIER'S EMPIRE-STYLE DESK IS SHOWN HERE IN THE WEST SITTING ROOM (LEFT) BELOW A CARZOU WATERCOLOR, *LE HOFGARTEN À BAYREUTH.*

THIS NINETEENTH-CENTURY
EMPIRE—STYLE SLANT FRONT
DESK (LEFT) WAS ONE OF JUST
A FEW ITEMS OWNED BY
JACKIE THAT PREVIOUSLY
BELONGED TO HER BELOVED
FATHER, JOHN B. BOUVIER.

"JACKS" WAS HER FATHER'S
PET, SHARING HIS PASSION FOR
HORSES AND PRACTICAL JOKES.
THEY ARE PICTURED
TOGETHER AT ONE OF JACKIE'S
RIDING EVENTS.

The Yellow Oval Room

Jackie furnished the Yellow Oval Room tastefully, creating a formal living room in the private quarters where she and the president could receive guests, entertain friends, and occasionally meet with dignitaries. Although her decorating tended to be formal, Jackie happily accommodated her husband's more relaxed style, keeping his comfort foremost in her mind. "A rocker is a rocker and there isn't much you can do to make it look like anything else," Jackie said as she moved rocking chairs into several of the White House rooms.

THESE 1815 GOLD PARIS PORCELAIN VASES WERE MOUNTED AS LAMPS AND FITTED FOR ELECTRICITY. THE BODIES OF THE LAMPS ARE SHAPED LIKE SHIELDS, DEPICTING A CLASSICAL MAIDEN AND WARRIOR. THEY SAT ATOP THE NUCLEAR TEST BAN TREATY DESK IN THE YELLOW OVAL ROOM.

LAMPS
ESTIMATE: $1,500
PRICE: $31,500

GRAMMY-AWARD-WINNING LYRICIST CAROL BAYER SAGER BOUGHT THIS ROCKING CHAIR, WHICH STOOD IN FRONT OF THE FIREPLACE IN THE YELLOW OVAL ROOM, FOR HER FIANCÉ AS A WEDDING GIFT. ANOTHER ROCKER, WHOSE ORIGINAL LOCATION WAS UNIDENTIFIED, SOLD FOR ONLY SLIGHTLY LESS, $442,500.

ROCKERS

The rocking chair, used to relieve JFK's chronic back pain, became a symbol of his presidency. There were rocking chairs in nearly every place JFK spent time.

1. Oval Office
2. JFK's secretary's office
3. Yellow Oval Room
4. JFK's bedroom
5. JKO's bedroom
6. GlenOra
7. Camp David
8. Hyannisport
9. Hammersmith Farm
10. West Palm Beach

JFK IN HIS ROCKER CHATTING WITH DR. ERICH MENDE, CHAIRMAN OF THE FREE DEMOCRATIC PARTY OF WEST GERMANY, MARCH, 1962.

ROCKER
ESTIMATE:
$3,500–5,000
PRICE:
$453,500

Nuclear Test Ban Treaty Desk

Jackie was extremely proud of all of her husband's accomplishments, as he was of hers. Theirs was a true partnership, in which each supported the other's achievements. One of the president's greatest was the negotiation of the Nuclear Test Ban Treaty. It was a monumental political event, and high excitement surrounded the historic signing.

On October 7, 1963, many people gathered in the newly restored Treaty Room to witness firsthand the president putting pen to paper to make the test ban official. The group was too large, however, to fit comfortably around the desk in the Treaty Room, so at the last minute a smaller desk from the Yellow Oval Room was brought in. This desk became a lasting symbol of peace and hope.

NUCLEAR TEST
BAN TREATY DESK
ESTIMATE:
$20,000-30,000
PRICE:
$1,432,500

JACKIE MOVED THE NUCLEAR TEST BAN TREATY DESK, PERHAPS THE MOST HISTORICALLY SIGNIFICANT ITEM IN THE ESTATE, TO HER NEW YORK CITY APARTMENT, WHERE IT BECAME HER PERSONAL DESK.

THE CUBAN MISSILE CRISIS OF OCTOBER 1962 HAD PUSHED THE SUPERPOWERS TO THE BRINK OF NUCLEAR WAR. IT WAS CLEAR THAT STEPS HAD TO BE TAKEN TO PREVENT THE SITUATION FROM RECURRING. PRESIDENT KENNEDY ORCHESTRATED A TENSE, TEN-DAY NEGOTIATION SESSION IN MOSCOW, WHICH RESULTED IN AN AGREEMENT AMONG THE UNITED STATES, THE SOVIET UNION, AND THE UNITED KINGDOM TO LIMIT THE TESTING OF ALL NUCLEAR WEAPONS.
PRESENT AT THE SIGNING CEREMONY WERE, FROM LEFT TO RIGHT: WILLIAM J. HOPKINS, WILLIAM FOSTER, JOHN MCCLOY, ADRIAN FISHER, SENATOR JOHN PASTORE, AVERILL HARRIMAN, SENATOR GEORGE SMATHERS, SENATOR WILLIAM FULBRIGHT, DEAN RUSK, SENATOR GEORGE AIKEN, SENATOR HUBERT HUMPHREY, SENATOR EVERETT DIRKSEN, SENATOR TOM KUCHEL, SENATOR HOWARD CANNON, LEVERETT SALTONSTALL, SENATOR HENRY JACKSON, AND VICE PRESIDENT LYNDON JOHNSON.

The Red Room

Of all the state rooms, the Red Room was Jackie's favorite. Dignified, elegant, and rich in history, it represented everything she did. Designed by Stephane Boudin under Jackie's well-trained eye, its rich wood, French neoclassical furniture and red twill satin walls reflected Jackie's refined taste perfectly. As an expression of her attachment to the room, Jackie placed her own French Empire obelisks on the mantel, a mantel that dates back to President Monroe's days, when it graced the state dining room.

WHEN JACKIE MOVED TO NEW YORK, THESE EIGHTEENTH-CENTURY LOUIS XVI OBELISKS MOVED WITH HER AND ADORNED THE MANTEL OF HER FIFTH AVENUE DINING ROOM. WITH ITS BOLD RED FLORAL WALLS AND MAJESTIC MARBLE FIREPLACE, HER DINING ROOM RESEMBLED HER FAVORITE WHITE HOUSE ROOM.

ALTERNATE BIDS

Among the unsuccessful bidders for the obelisks was a White House representative who was also interested in obtaining the Elaine de Kooning sketch of JFK, the Nuclear Test Ban Treaty desk, and an Aaron Shikler study for his White House portrait of Jackie. Using money donated by the White House Historical Association, she was ultimately successful in purchasing a sketch entitled *Miss Lane's Reception at the White House.* It is currently in the Curator's Office at the White House.

❧

LOUIS XVI OBELISKS
ESTIMATE:
$10,000–15,000
PRICE: $85,500

JACKIE'S OBELISKS MESHED PERFECTLY WITH THE RED ROOM'S FINE WOODS AND NEOCLASSICAL CURVES.

The President's Bedroom

These paintings, a gift from Jackie, were the only furnishings from the president's White House bedroom—where they hung on either side of the mantel—included in the estate auction. Oil on canvas, the pair of paintings are officially titled "Smolensko Ahead" and "A Chestnut Colt with Jockey Up."

PAIR OF PAINTINGS
ESTIMATE:
$2,000-3,000
PRICE: $74,000

A VIEW OF THE PRESIDENT'S BEDROOM
AND ANOTHER SHOWING ONE
OF HIS FAMOUS ROCKING CHAIRS (INSET).

Portrait of John F. Kennedy by Elaine de Kooning

Between Christmas 1962 and New Year's Day 1963, Elaine de Kooning sketched the president in West Palm Beach. Years later, when writing of this time, Mrs. de Kooning recounted, "Everyone is familiar with the quick sense of humor revealed in the corners of his mouth and the laugh lines around the eyes, but what impressed me the most was a sense of compassion." She perfectly captured both this compassionate character and JFK's carefree confidence.

THE PORTRAIT THAT ELAINE DE KOONING PAINTED OF JFK FOR THE TRUMAN LIBRARY WAS ONE OF HER LAST; SHE SUBSEQUENTLY DEDICATED HER TIME SOLELY TO SCULPTURE.

DE KOONING
PORTRAIT
ESTIMATE:
$3,000–4,000
PRICE: $101,500

Five Least Expensive Items

These were the five lots that fetched the lowest price at the auction.

1. Six volumes about Asia
ESTIMATE: $100–150
PRICE: $1,437

2. *Les Grande Meaulnes*
by Henri Alain-Fournier
ESTIMATE: 300-500
PRICE: $1,725

3. *Harold Macmillan, Volume I, 1894–1956,*
by Alistair Horne
Inscribed, "With every best wish and many grateful thanks for your help on vol. II, Alistair Horne, Newport R.I. 27/3/89."
ESTIMATE: $200–300
PRICE: $1,955

4. *Unless the Grain Die*
Texts by Saint Augustine of Hippo and Saint Ignatius of Antioch
ESTIMATE: $200-400
PRICE: $1,955

5. Print of Washington, D.C.
ESTIMATE: $20–30
PRICE: $2,070

Five Most Expensive Items

Far more celebrated, these are the five items that sold for the highest prices at the auction.

1. Lesotho III Diamond
ESTIMATE: $500,000–600,000
PRICE: $2,587,500

2. Nuclear Test Ban Treaty Desk
ESTIMATE: $20,000–30,000
PRICE: $1,432,500

3. MacGregor Woods (golf clubs)
ESTIMATE: $700–900
PRICE: $772,500

4. Humidor
ESTIMATE: $2,000–2,500
PRICE: $574,500

5. Oak Rocker
ESTIMATE: $3,000–5,000
PRICE: $453,500

Family Portraits

"I would like to remember them at this age. As they are, just now," Jackie explained to portraitist Aaron Shikler when he first came to her home. It was 1967, Caroline was ten and John seven, and Jackie had commissioned Mr. Shikler to paint her children's portraits. He suspects she chose him because she had admired portraits he had done of the Lawford children, her nieces and nephews.

The artist came to sketch the children in the late afternoon, after they arrived home from school, in the familiar, comfortable setting of their home. He fondly remembers Caroline "often in a nightgown with a book in her hand, being a born model. Pausing in a doorway, cross-legged on the floor, nose in a book, questioning her mother, she was always spontaneous, unrehearsed, always a painting." John Jr., he recounts, was "all boy, restless, impatient, all elbows and knees. He was monumentally bored with the whole business; his most frequent comment was a groan."

In 1968, after Jackie was asked by the White House to provide a painting of herself for permanent display there, she again turned to Mr. Shikler. The two had worked well together; she respected his integrity as an artist and never attempted to influence his work. He sketched her in numerous poses, both formal and casual, explaining, "I needed to paint picture of the First Lady of the land at the same time that I painted a picture of Jacqueline Bouvier Kennedy." One of the sketches was of Jackie sprawled on the couch in slacks, and they both laughed at the thought of the reaction such a pose would meet from the powers in Washington. The pose he finally chose was Jacqueline Kennedy standing in a full-length off-white dress before the fireplace in her living room. He wanted a "brighter, less troubled image, one that would evoke how he and the rest of the country saw her; as an ethereal woman of almost mythological dimensions." The portrait was unveiled in 1971 and hangs in the Vermeil Room of the White House.

In the end, Shikler's studies for the White House portrait of Jacqueline Kennedy and his studies of her children sold for more than $1.2 million.

STUDY OF CAROLINE KENNEDY (TOP); STUDY OF CAROLINE (MIDDLE LEFT); STUDY OF JOHN JR. (MIDDLE RIGHT); STUDY OF CAROLINE AND JOHN JR. (BOTTOM).

STUDY FOR THE WHITE HOUSE
portrait of Jacqueline Kennedy.

STUDY OF JACKIE
ESTIMATE:
$10,000–15,000
PRICE: $184,000

⌇⌇⌇

STUDY OF CAROLINE
ESTIMATE:
$2,000–3,000
PRICE: $10,350

⌇⌇⌇

STUDY OF CAROLINE
ESTIMATE:
$1,500–2,500
PRICE: $25,300

⌇⌇⌇

STUDY OF JOHN JR.
ESTIMATE:
$1,500–2,500
PRICE: $24,150

⌇⌇⌇

STUDY OF CAROLINE
AND JOHN JR.
ESTIMATE:
$2,000–3,000
PRICE: $54,625

On March 14, 1962, President Kennedy hosted a White House reception for Peter Tare, an organization of people who served on PT boats. The group gave the president several gifts, some of which are on display at the Kennedy Museum. This Tiffany gold key (left), inscribed "109," was one gift that Jackie kept.

PT 109 Memorabilia

Just the mention of this famous World War II boat immediately calls to mind images of the young Jack Kennedy risking his own life to save his shipmates. Many books were written commemorating the event, and Hollywood made a movie about the famous rescue, aptly called *PT 109*.

JFK collaborated closely with one author, Robert Donovan, on his book *PT 109: John F. Kennedy in WWII*. A copy of the book was part of a lot auctioned for $6,325.

CORAL SCULPTURE
ESTIMATE:
$8,000–12,000
PRICE: $68,500

GOLD KEY
ESTIMATE:
$200–300
PRICE: $34,500

IN A SENTIMENTAL PRESENTATION, MR. DONOVAN GAVE THE PRESIDENT A PIECE OF CORAL FROM THE ISLAND IN THE SOUTH PACIFIC WHERE HE WAS SHIPWRECKED. JEWELRY DESIGNER DAVID WEBB INTEGRATED THE PIECE OF CORAL INTO THIS SCULPTURE.

The Ultimate Cigar Aficionado

In what was certainly the most perfect match between object and purchaser, Marvin Shanken, publisher of *Cigar Aficionado*, walked away with President Kennedy's humidor. He reflected on the now-famous evening in a recent edition of his magazine:

"…The only thing I knew was that I wanted President John F. Kennedy's humidor, a present to him from Milton Berle on JFK's inauguration day in 1961.

"In the midst of the crowd, waiting for the last lot of the evening to come up for bidding, the importance of the moment dawned on me. This wasn't just about a humidor, it was about a piece of history.

"Kennedy ranks with Winston Churchill as one of the great cigar-smoking statesmen of our time. Furthermore, his decision to impose the trade embargo on Cuba forever linked him, even more closely, with the subject that remains dear to cigar lovers. When you also consider that I publish *Cigar Aficionado*, it was entirely natural that the humidor end up in the magazine's office.

"It's a beautiful humidor. It's much larger than I expected, in part because the dimensions published in the Sotheby's catalogue were incorrect; instead of 12½ inches long, it is

THE FAMOUS HUMIDOR (ABOVE) IS SEEN ON THE AUCTION BLOCK; HAPPY PURCHASER MARVIN SHANKEN (RIGHT) CELEBRATES BY LIGHTING UP.

HUMIDOR
ESTIMATE: $2,000–2,500
PRICE: $574,500

THE PRESIDENT IS SEEN HERE RELAXING ON THE *HONEYFITZ*, THE PRESIDENTIAL YACHT.

21½ inches. Milton Berle had Alfred Dunhill of London make the walnut box for the president. He told me it cost about $800–1,000 at the time—a considerable sum of money back then. It bears a small plaque from Milton that reads, 'To J.F.K. Good Health—Good Smoking. Milton Berle, 1/20/61.'

"All of those thoughts rumbled into my head as the bidding started. While I was conscious of the numbers rapidly climbing, I waited until the bids were well over $100,000 before bidding. Hands kept flying up all around me until the bids reached about $250,000. Finally it was down to me and a phone bidder from Chicago. At $400,000 there was a long pause from the phone bidder. I instinctively knew we were at or near his limit; I had passed mine minutes before so I was already be-yond caring about the amount. Now it was about the humidor.

"As he made his next bid, I knew in my gut that we were entering un-charted price territory. Bidding quickly moved from $400,000 to $500,000. His $510,000 had been pre-ceded by another long pause. I then bid $520,000 and waited. Almost in a dream, I heard the gavel slam down and the auctioneer say, 'Sold!' amid the cheers in the room. Not knowing who I was, auctioneer Diana Brooks, the president and CEO of Sotheby's, said from the podium, 'I hope you like cigars.' Little did she know!

"The humidor, and all that it means to cigar smokers who revere President John F. Kennedy, is now preserved. *Cigar Aficionado* has now become the guardian of an impor-tant symbol, a legacy of JFK's love of a fine cigar. It is an honor."

JFK ENJOYS ANOTHER CIGAR WHILE STROLLING IN **HYANNIS**.

The President's Golf Clubs

Though Jack Kennedy liked to play golf, during his presidency his back pain, coupled with his busy schedule, didn't allow much time for it. He played golf only three times while in office, all during the summer of 1963. On one outing in Hyannis in July he was joined by Paul "Red" Fay, a friend of JFK's from PT training school.(After becoming president, JFK appointed him Undersecretary of the Navy. An edition of his book, *The Pleasure of His Company*, poignantly inscribed "For Jackie, with Respect, Humility and Affection, Red. 1 Sept. 1966," was sold at the auction for

AVID GOLFERS, CELEBRITIES, AND MEMORABILIA BUFFS BATTLED IT OUT BEFORE AN UNLIKELY WINNER WALKED AWAY WITH JFK'S MACGREGOR WOODS: ARNOLD SCHWARZENEGGER, MARRIED TO JFK'S NIECE, MARIA SHRIVER. MANY WONDERED WHY ARNOLD HADN'T SIMPLY ASKED CAROLINE OR JOHN, WITH WHOM HE IS FRIENDLY, FOR THEM. SURELY HE RECOGNIZED THAT THEY WERE COMPLYING WITH THEIR MOTHER'S WISHES, AND THAT TO DIVIDE HER POSSESSIONS AMONG OVER EIGHTY COUSINS WOULD BE NEARLY IMPOSSIBLE.

JACK IS PICTURED HERE DURING HIS
NEWPORT OUTING WITH BEN BRADLEE
OF THE *WASHINGTON POST*. JACKIE AND
TONI BRADLEE FOLLOW BEHIND,
ENGAGED IN CONVERSATION.

$12,650.) Later that summer President Kennedy played again in Hyannis, with Pierre Salinger, Lem Billings, and David Ormsby Gore.

In September Jack and Jackie spent their tenth wedding anniversary weekend at Hammersmith Farm in Newport, celebrating with a small group of friends and family. Over the course of the weekend the president and his good friend Ben Bradlee took to the course, accompanied by their wives.

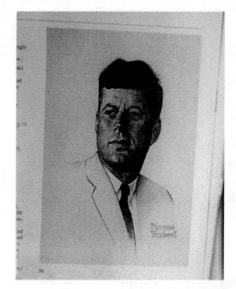

IN ADDITION TO THE GOLF CLUBS, ARNOLD SCHWARZENEGGER ALSO BOUGHT THIS PORTRAIT OF JFK BY NORMAN ROCKWELL (ABOVE) FOR $134,500, AS WELL AS A LEATHER DESK SET FOR $189,500.

OUTBID

Waving his paddle until the very end, Long Island businessman Don Carter dropped out of the bidding at $690,00, saying that he knew the phone bidder (Arnold) was prepared to go to a million dollars. Boston Red Sox pitcher Roger Clemens was another unsuccessful bidder; he had asked permission to leave the dugout midway through a game so he could bid on the clubs, making his phone calls from the team doctor's office. He dropped out at $121,000.

Jackie's Jewelry

⸻⦵⸻

That Jackie had the panache of a star was evident from the time she was a young woman. Her exotic features and regal bearing brought her international attention as First Lady. Simple, elegant, beautiful, the quintessential "Jackie look" was admired and copied the world over.

The national obsession with Jackie's appearance was unprecedented; she set trends as no other First Lady had before, or has since. Her wardrobe consisted mainly of solid-color suits in sumptuous fabrics, sleeveless, form-fitting A-line dresses, and simple gowns with geometric necklines. Jackie's outfits were so stunning in their simplicity that they rarely needed to be accessorized. When Jackie did choose to accent an outfit, it was usually with simple ear clips and faux pearls.

The jewels that Jackie received and wore while married to Aristotle Onassis differed from the simple, classic jewelry she purchased for herself. They were more a reflection of Ari's abounding generosity than of Jackie's personal taste. Yet from the opulent rubies Ari gave her to the simple strands of beads she so loved, Jackie looked ravishing in anything that adorned her.

JACKIE'S JEWELS ON DISPLAY AT SOTHEBY'S, NEW YORK.

The Pearls

Jackie loved pearls. She had many strands that she enjoyed wearing, but these were the pearls that defined her. Is it any wonder that Sotheby's chose this photograph to depict Jackie? This is the image ensconced in the hearts and minds of America.

THE PHOTO OF JOHN JR. TUGGING AT HIS MOTHER'S PEARLS (LEFT) HAS BECOME ONE OF THE MOST LASTING IMAGES OF THE AUCTION.

JACKIE (ABOVE) STUDYING PLANS FOR THE PRESERVATION OF LAFAYETTE SQUARE IN WASHINGTON, D.C.

THE PEARLS
ESTIMATE:
$500–700
PRICE:
$211,500

A FEELING OF AWE FILLED THE ROOM WHEN THESE PEARLS WERE BROUGHT ONTO THE AUCTION BLOCK.

MINT CONDITION

The Franklin Mint purchased Jackie's famous pearls and plans to display them at their museum. They are also marketing a reproduction of the necklace. "Of all the items available at the auction, we felt this necklace best represented Jackie's style and spirit," said a spokesperson for the Mint. She wore it everywhere. At the beach in Hyannisport, with her family, greeting royalty, and at state dinners. This triple-strand pearl necklace is an American classic, like the woman who wore it.

FROM STABLE TO SALON—JACKIE TOURING HICKORY HILL (RIGHT), THE HOME OF ROBERT AND ETHEL KENNEDY, HOSTING AN ALUMNAE RECEPTION (BELOW) AT MISS PORTER'S SCHOOL, AND CAPTURED IN A CLASSICALLY ALLURING PORTRAIT (LEFT).

A Favorite Necklace

Jackie could conjure up the appropriate look for any occasion. This was the necklace she wore when she proudly stood by her husband's side as he announced his presidential candidacy. The Black "Stone" Necklace could be converted from a single to a double strand, and she wore it from the campaign trail to the White House and beyond.. Simple and versatile, it perfectly complemented Jackie's classic attire.

Jackie wore this necklace when she first met and enchanted President Charles de Gaulle of France, and fittingly, these beads will be returning to the country that Jackie so loved. The necklace was purchased by a French clothing company, Gerard Darel. Their advertising tag line is "The Story of Charm." As Danielle Darel points out, "Mrs. Onassis was the representation of charm."

BLACK "STONE"
NECKLACE
ESTIMATE:
$200-300
PRICE: $101,500

JACKIE IS PICTURED (FAR RIGHT) WEARING THE NECKLACE ON OCTOBER 5, 1961, WHILE BEING PRESENTED WITH A TICKET TO THE NATIONAL SYMPHONY.

THE EVER-VERSATILE NECKLACE APPEARS AGAIN (RIGHT) ON DECEMBER 16, 1961, UPON JACKIE'S ARRIVAL IN SAN JUAN, PUERTO RICO.

Costume Jewelry

Much of Jackie's jewelry collection comprised "fashion" or costume pieces. During the auction, it didn't matter if it was real or fake, only that it was Jackie's.

Famed costume jewelry designer Kenneth Jay Lane recalled, "Jackie had been wearing my jewelry since the middle 1960s. When one day she asked me if I would do her a favor, I of course said yes. The 'favor' was to make a near replica of a wonderful Van Cleef necklace that Ari had given her.

"I went to tea at 1040, where Jackie had taken the necklace out of the bank to show me. To offset the price of the duplication I asked if I could sell it as part of my collection. With her blessing, I have produced the necklace and used the motifs in every possible manner for the past twenty-five years. One day Jackie said to me in her wonderful whisper, 'Kenny, I saw our necklace again on *Dynasty*.'"

COSTUME EAR CLIPS AND NECKLACE—A PERFECT SUITE.

COSTUME JEWELRY
ESTIMATE:
$1,000–1,500
PRICE:
$90,500

THESE EAR CLIPS, FASHIONED BY KENNETH JAY LANE, WERE PART OF A LOT OF COSTUME JEWELRY THAT SOLD FOR $90,500.

A Perfect Bag

Like every woman, Jackie had her favorite accessories. Whether dining with heads of state or greeting entertainers, she always carried a clutch bag. Perfectly complementing her signature white-gloved hands, the bag was tasteful, discreet, always just right.

Jackie's use of envelope-shaped pocketbooks brought them into vogue, as American women mimicked her every move.

THIS 18-KARAT-GOLD BASKET-WEAVE VAN CLEEF & ARPELS BAG HAD AN INTERIOR LIPSTICK CASE AND MIRROR.

A BAG FOR ALL SEASONS—WHITE HOUSE DINNER HONORING ANDRÉ MALRAUX (FAR LEFT), MAY, 1962; THE KENNEDYS IN MEXICO CITY (UPPER LEFT), JUNE, 1962; AT A STATE DINNER HONORING THE PRESIDENT OF SUDAN (LOWER LEFT), OCTOBER, 1961.

GOLD BAG
ESTIMATE:
$2,000–3,000
PRICE:
$68,500

Aristotle's Gifts

Aristotle Onassis first met Jackie in 1963 when she and her sister Lee Radziwill spent time vacationing aboard his yacht, the *Christina*. He was enamored of her beauty, wit, and grace. Years later, when their paths crossed again, he courted her and eventually proposed.

Aristotle Onassis, one of the wealthiest men the world had ever known, carried a diamond ring in his pocket on the night he went to propose to John F. Kennedy's widow—a 40.42-carat marquise-shaped diamond. What more could Ari do to sweep this most dazzling of women off her feet but offer one of the largest diamonds in the world?

Ari had a penchant for buying jewelry. Several days prior to his wedding to Jackie, he visited Zolotas,

JACKIE IS SEEN HERE WITH ARISTOTLE HAVING FUN AT HER FORTIETH BIRTHDAY PARTY, WEARING THE MOON EAR CLIPS THAT HE HAD GIVEN HER TWO DAYS BEFORE.

ARI COMMISSIONED GREEK
JEWELRY DESIGNER ILIAS
LALAOUNIS TO CREATE A PAIR
OF "MOON EAR CLIPS" FOR HIS
WIFE, TO COMMEMORATE THE
FIRST MOON LANDING IN 1969.
EACH MOON IS CREATED FROM
HAMMERED GOLD, AND THE
SURFACE IS DOTTED WITH
CRATERS OF RUBIES. THEY
HANG FROM LINKS SHAPED LIKE
SPACE CAPSULES, SUSPENDED
FROM CIRCLING ROCKETS.

MOON EAR CLIPS
ESTIMATE:
$1,000–1,200
PRICE:
$112,500

his favorite Athens jewelry store, where he made many purchases. After the wedding ceremony, amid the revelry of the wedding reception aboard the *Christina*, Ari presented his new bride with over $1 million worth of rubies. He also bought "party favors" for the other guests in the form of gold bracelets, a diamond pin for Jackie's mom, and other "trinkets." In all, Ari gave Jackie jewels worth more than $5 million over the course of their four-year marriage.

LESOTHO III

The room was hushed when the diamond first appeared on the auction block, but the quiet soon turned into exuberant banter. The bidding was fast and furious, jumping in ten-thousand-dollar increments by the split second. In a matter of minutes it went to a million and the crowd sat up in their seats; one and a half million, and they cooed; two million, and they applauded. At two and a half million the Sotheby's audience erupted in cheers.

When the gavel came down for the last time, the Greek tycoon's engagement gift belonged to the daughter of one of his old business rivals. In a symbolic transaction, Anthony O'Reilly, chairman of HJ Heinz, purchased the diamond for his wife's birthday. The parallels are uncanny: Chryssanthie Goulandris is an heiress to the Goulandris shipping empire. While her family and the Onassis clan were business rivals, they were also friends. She, like Jackie, is an avid horse lover, raising champion thoroughbreds. Mr. O'Reilly, Dublin-born and owner of Wedgwood Waterford, is revered in his home country, much as the people of the Emerald Isle once revered JFK.

In May of 1967, in Lesotho, South Africa, Ernestine Ramaboa uncovered the largest diamond ever to be found by a woman. Hiding it under her skirt, she ran back to the hut she shared with her husband, a diamond digger. Eventually the diamond found its way to New York City, where famed jeweler Harry Winston held a press conference to showcase the diamond to the public. Before it was cut it was exhibited at the Smithsonian Institute in Washington, D.C., as well as the Museum of Natural History in New York. Jackie's marquis-shaped stone was the third largest to be cut from the rough diamond, hence the name Lesotho III.

DIAMOND RING

ESTIMATE:
$500,000–600,000
PRICE:
$2,587,500

This ruby necklace (left) is designed in a floral motif with diamond petals surrounding ruby centers. The total diamond weight is approximately 35 carats.

These spectacular ruby earrings (below) were one of Jackie's wedding gifts from Ari, and she continued to wear them for years. She was photographed with them (right) in December, 1988, at a party at CBS in tribute to William Paley. The top part consists of large "leaves" set with approximately 14 carats worth of diamonds. The ruby pendants total nearly 76 carats.

The heart-shaped ruby ring (bottom) is surrounded by approximately 3 carats of diamonds.

Ruby Earrings
Estimate: $25,000–35,000
Price: $360,000

Ruby Necklace
Estimate: $75,000–100,000
Price: $250,000

Ruby Ring
Estimate: $4,000
Price: $101,500

Special Ear Clips

Jackie's desire to preserve her husband's place in history led to the creation of the Kennedy Library. She selected the spot, overlooking his beloved Boston Harbor, and personally oversaw the design of this awesome building, which opened in 1979. After nearly fifteen years of service the library was ready for a face-lift. Under the design direction of Caroline Kennedy's husband, Edward Schlossberg, the Kennedy Library and Museum reopened to much fanfare on October 29, 1993.

It was a glorious event, attended by President Bill Clinton as well as numerous members of the Kennedy clan. It's difficult to determine whose attention the media was vying for more, Jackie's or the president's. Thirty years after her magical reign, Jackie still had the ability to stop people in their tracks. At sixty, she had taken on a mature and sophisticated look, but her grandeur was still there. This was a happy day, and everyone's hearts were full. No one knew it would be Jackie's last visit to the museum she created.

THESE HEART-SHAPED 18-KARAT YELLOW AND WHITE GOLD EARRINGS, TASTEFUL IN THEIR SIMPLICITY, WERE APPROPRIATE FOR ANY OCCASION. SHE IS SEEN HERE WEARING THEM AT THE REDEDICATION CEREMONY FOR THE KENNEDY LIBRARY IN 1993, SHARING THE WARMTH OF THE DAY WITH HER CHILDREN AND PRESIDENT CLINTON.

EAR CLIPS
ESTIMATE: $3,000–4,000
PRICE: $37,375

Arts and Leisure

⎯⎯⎯∞∞∞⎯⎯⎯

Jackie's love of the arts and literature graced every aspect of her life. From her childhood through her years as First Lady and her career as a book editor, the common thread that ran through Jackie's life was her love of words, art, and music.

Jackie was passionate about art. Her taste was eclectic and clearly displayed the breadth of her interests. She didn't consider herself a connoisseur, but Jackie filled her home with artwork that, quite simply, she liked to look at. Nevertheless, her discerning eye certainly chose some significant pieces.

In her Fifth Avenue apartment Jackie displayed numerous nature prints, many of which had previously hung in the White House. Her sculpture collection included pieces that dated back to the third and fourth centuries B.C. Greek and Roman marble busts lent a classical presence to her living room, and bronze and terra-cotta figurines of gods and goddesses adorned tables throughout her home. Jackie had an ardent interest in India, perhaps stemming from her memorable trip there as First Lady. Her book collection reflected her desire to learn more about this mythical land, and among her treasures were dozens of Indian miniatures, many of them illustrated histories commemorating events in the lives of Indian rulers, while others reflected scenes from palace life.

Jackie combined varied art works with flair. In her living room a John Singer Sargent rested on an easel next to a table supporting marble busts. Pastel portraits of her children hung near Japanese marble candlesticks. On Jackie's foyer table sat an ancient Greek vase, and above hung nineteenth century French watercolors.

Jackie was something of an artist herself. Though she would say she dabbled, her skills were beyond amateur. She began sketching as a child, doodling in notebooks and creating children's stories. As an adult she would often take out her paintbrushes on summer afternoons in Hyannisport, and in her New York apartment she set up a large easel next to a window overlooking Central Park.

JACKIE'S FIFTH AVENUE APARTMENT BUIDING.

Watercolors by John Singer Sargent

Jackie greatly admired the work of John Singer Sargent, and purchased two of his watercolors, both of which she displayed in her living room. These were among the most highly valued items in the auction.

 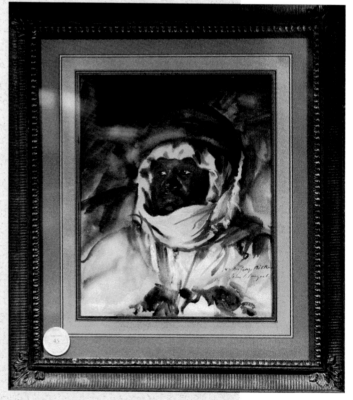

VENETIAN GIRL (LEFT) WAS INSPIRED BY ONE OF JOHN SINGER SARGENT'S MANY TRIPS TO VENICE. IT ORIGINALLY BELONGED TO HIS SISTER, EMILY. *HEAD OF AN ARAB* (RIGHT) WAS PAINTED DURING THE ARTIST'S TRIP THROUGH SYRIA AND PALESTINE IN 1905–06. JACKIE PURCHASED BOTH WORKS IN 1969.

Marie Antoinette's Leather Box

Jackie was no stranger to auctions, as portions of her vast collection of artwork and sculpture had been acquired in this way. In 1981 Jackie purchased this box, which was once Marie Antoinette's, at an auction. Perhaps she had the same feeling about owning something that belonged to this French legend as many had about owning of Jackie's. John Mass, the London–based antiques dealer who purchased the box for an American client, summed it up best: "If you wanted the best provenance of two women in the world, it would be Marie Antoinette and Jackie Kennedy."

FRANCE'S LEGENDARY FIRST LADY, MARIE ANTOINETTE.

RED LEATHER BOX
ESTIMATE:
$25,000–35,000
PRICE:
$118,000

LOUIS XV GILT-TOOLED RED MOROCCO LEATHER CASKET, CIRCA 1770.

309

Equestrian Portraits

Like most equestrians, Jackie loved everything about horses and filled her home with images of them. She had dozens of sketches, photos, and oil paintings of these majestic animals. These works captured the integrity of the horse—proud, spirited, regal. It is easy to see why Jackie felt an affinity with these animals.

Over fifty pieces featuring horses and equestrian themes were included in the estate sale.

THE MOST FAMOUS AND HIGHLY VALUED OF THE LOT WAS JOHN WOOTTON'S *LORD BATEMAN'S ARABIAN*, DATED 1733–34.

AN IMPORTANT EQUESTRIAN CANVAS, *A BAY HORSE IN A LANDSACAPE WITH GROOM, SAID TO BE FLYING "CHILDERS,"* ATTRIBUTED TO THE CIRCLE OF JOHN WOOTTON.

LORD BATEMAN'S ARABIAN

ESTIMATE:
$80,000–120,000
PRICE: $343,500

—☙—

A BAY HORSE IN A LANDSCAPE WITH GROOM, SAID TO BE FLYING "CHILDERS"

ESTIMATE:
$30,000–40,000
PRICE: $40,250

PICTURED IN THE SOTHEBY'S SHOWROOM ABOVE IS A LOUIS XVI-STYLE RED LEATHER
COUCH (SOLD FOR $11,500) AND *AN EQUESTRIAN PORTRAIT OF A NOBLEMAN* BY JOHANN
GEORGE DE HAMILTON. JACKIE DISPLAYED THE PAINTING IN THE DINING ROOM OF HER
FIFTH AVENUE APARTMENT. SHE PURCHASED IT AT AUCTION FROM SOTHEBY'S, LONDON,
IN JULY, 1986. AT THE ONASSIS AUCTION IT SOLD FOR $79,500.

A Love of Words

Jackie's love affair with books spanned a lifetime. Many of her teachers commented that as a young girl she had the most inquisitive mind they had ever encountered in a child. History was her passion, but Jackie also read the classics, was fluent in French and Spanish, and always yearned to learn more about the arts. She turned to books to fuel her deepening intelligence and imagination.

As a teen away at school, she would often retire to her room to read in the evening while the other girls gathered to gossip and giggle. While on the grueling campaign trail with JFK, Jackie would sometimes retreat to the back of the plane, put her feet up, and open a book.

As First Lady, Jackie brought her love of literature to the White House. At perhaps the most famous White House gathering, in April of 1962, Jackie invited such esteemed authors as William Styron and James Baldwin to a dinner honoring Nobel Prize winners. JFK's summation of the event has become as notable as the evening itself—"I think this is the most extraordinary collection of talent, of human knowledge, that has ever been gathered together in the White House, with the possible exception of when Thomas Jefferson dined alone."

The end of the 1970s found Jackie firmly settled in New York City, her children grown, ready to enter a new phase of her life. The world of publishing was a natural choice, drawing on her lifelong passion.

JACKIE'S NUMEROUS BOOKS ON DISPLAY AT SOTHEBY'S, NEW YORK.

"To me, a wonderful book is one that takes me on a journey into something I didn't know before."

—JKO

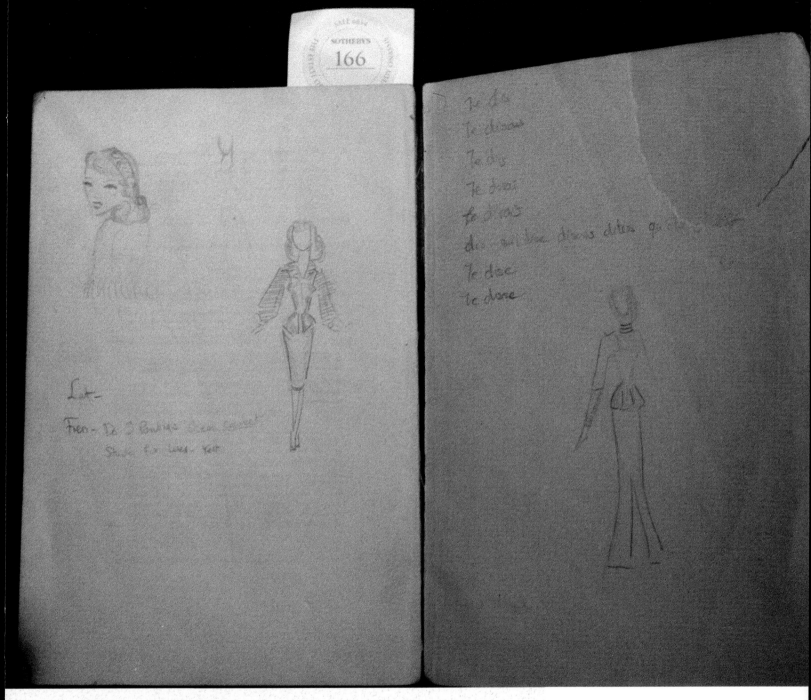

THIS TEXTBOOK, *COMPLETE TREATISE ON THE CONJUGATION OF VERBS*, WHICH JACKIE HAD SAVED FROM HER CHILDHOOD, CONTAINED NOT ONLY SCHOOLWORK BUT A FAIR AMOUNT OF DOODLING.

As a book editor Jackie was a visionary, and a deep and true appreciation for the arts shone through in all of her projects. She brought to life many books that bear the mark of a gifted, involved, and keenly interested editor.

It was Jackie who championed the cause of Naguib Mafouz, the Egyptian Nobel Prize winner, in America, having read his book in its French translation. She coaxed a reluctant Bill Moyers to create *World of Ideas*, which went on to sell nearly 1 million copies. *The Last Tsar*, which struck a chord with Jackie's keen interest in Russian history, also became a surprise bestseller, largely because of her energetic enthusiasm. Jackie fell in love with her projects, and nurtured them as a mother does a growing child.

At Doubleday, Jackie's colleagues were reverential but by no means overawed. Allowed to preserve an anonymity that made her comfortable, she participated in editorial meetings and chatted in the elevator just like any other employee.

Those who knew her best immediately associated Jackie with her love of books. John said it best in his first public appearance after his mother's death; "She was with the people and things she loved, her books." When choosing the readings for their mother's funeral service, John and Caroline took care to make selections that would reflect "her

love of words, her spirit of adventure, and the bonds of family."

Jackie filled her home with the books she so loved. In her apartment, floor-to-ceiling bookshelves burst with volumes, and books were stacked on tables, under tables, in virtually every room. Of all her riches these were her most cherished, and nowhere was her brilliant and inquisitive mind more evident.

The estate contained thousands of volumes, collected over a lifetime. Virtually everyone who wrote a memoir of JFK's administration presented Jackie with a copy, many inscribed with words of affection. Her love of the beach was preserved in volumes on Cape Cod and Martha's Vineyard. There were dozens of children's books on John F. Kennedy, over twenty volumes on Robert F. Kennedy, and books on fox hunting, interior design, poetry, and Greek and French literature. Jackie's books told the story of her life.

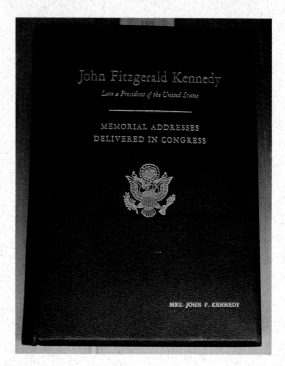

JOHN F. KENNEDY MEMORIAL ADDRESSES, DELIVERED IN CONGRESS. TRIBUTES IN EULOGY OF JOHN F. KENNEDY.

IN THE SALE WAS A GROUP OF APPROXIMATELY 250 MAGAZINES THAT JACKIE HAD COLLECTED OVER THE YEARS, EACH FEATURING PHOTOGRAPHS AND ARTICLES ON JACKIE KENNEDY AND HER FAMILY. THEY SPANNED THE 1960S THROUGH THE 1980S AND INCLUDED ISSUES OF *LIFE*, *PEOPLE*, *TIME*, *COSMOPOLITAN*, AND *LADIES' HOME JOURNAL*.

PROFILES IN COURAGE.
A MEMORIAL EDITION,
SPECIALLY BOUND
AND PRESENTED TO
MRS. KENNEDY.

PROFILES IN COURAGE

This volume, the first of
two specially bound copies of
the Memorial Edition of
"Profiles in Courage",
is presented by
the publisher to
Mrs. John F. Kennedy

JFK Memorial Addresses
ESTIMATE: $3,000–5,000
PRICE: $34,500

Magazines
ESTIMATE: $100–200
PRICE: $12,650

Profiles in Courage
ESTIMATE: $400–600
PRICE: $18,400

Baby Grand Piano

Of course Jackie's home had a piano, though Jackie didn't play. It needed refinishing and one of the foot pedals was broken, but that couldn't detract from its importance. The sleek black baby grand sat in Jackie's living room, with flowers, photos, and sculpture arranged on top.

As First Lady, Jackie was committed to giving America's youth a greater appreciation for music and she invited young musicians from across the nation to perform at the White House. This inspiring event was often a turning point for the performers, many of whom went on to pursue careers in music and credit Jackie for encouraging their success.

PIANO
ESTIMATE:
$3,000–5,000
PRICE:
$167,000

AFTER HER CAR, THIS PIANO, MADE BY HENRY F. MILLER OF BOSTON, WAS THE LARGEST OBJECT IN THE AUCTION, COMMANDING QUITE A PRESENCE IN SOTHEBY'S SHOWROOM. MRS. PAT BAKER OF MILWAUKEE, SEEING IT IN THE CATALOG, SENSED THAT IT WAS MEANT TO BE HERS, AND SHE BOARDED A PLANE TO NEW YORK TO BID ON IT. MRS. BAKER PURCHASED THE PIANO AS A GIFT FOR HER HUSBAND, AND THE INSTRUMENT IS NOW THE CENTERPIECE OF THEIR FLORIDA LIVING ROOM.

A True Equestrian

Every little girl loves horses, and Jackie was no exception. Long before "Macaroni" took up residence in the White House, horses were a big part of Jackie's life. From the time she was five years old, little Jackie Bouvier competed in horse shows on Long Island. Pigtails flying, she entered the ring proud and excited. One of her teachers said that she "thrived on competition, often performing better in the actual horse show than in the practice sessions." In an often tumultuous childhood, riding provided Jackie with a happy stability. Many of her happiest childhood memories were of the time she spent on horseback.

Jackie didn't outgrow her childhood love, and over time she became quite an accomplished rider. She was tender and affectionate with horses; a true equestrian. Riding provided Jackie with a sense of freedom that was difficult to find anywhere else as First Lady, and she rode as often as she could during those years.

Jackie passed her love of horses on to her children, teaching them to ride at a very young age. During their summers at Hyannisport, they spent many hours at the nearby stables,

SWISS–MADE SADDLE (MONOGRAMMED)
ESTIMATE: $300-500
PRICE: $90,500

ITALIAN–MADE SADDLE
ESTIMATE: $300-500
PRICE: $46,000

BOSTON–MADE SADDLE
ESTIMATE: $300-500
PRICE: $34,500

where grandfather Joseph Kennedy (also an avid rider) kept horses. Caroline took to horsemanship immediately and continued taking lessons in later years at the Claremont Riding Academy in New York. John also became a competent rider, and he and his mother competed in family riding events at his school.

After Jackie moved to New York, she would occasionally go riding in Central Park. She also kept a home in New Jersey horse country, spending many spring and fall weekends there. Several of Jackie's saddles were part of the sale. To a true equestrian, nothing could have been more "personally Jackie's" than these.

Jackie riding Saraan (above), a gift from President Kahn of Pakistan.

Jackie, always dashing, cut an especially fine figure (opposite page) in her riding outfits.

Jackie is riding with John and Caroline at GlenOra, the country home the Kennedys rented in Middleburg, Virginia, in the fall of 1962. Having enjoyed their time at GlenOra so much and anticipating a second term, in 1963 the Kennedys built a family retreat of their own. Named after President Kennedy's ancestral home in Ireland, Wexford became the weekend home where Jackie spent mornings on horseback.

"For our mother, history came alive through objects and paintings, as well as books. Because the things she collected link her with history, and because she cared about them, they represent more than just a record of her life and travels. As they go out into the world, we hope that they bring with them not only their own beauty and spirit, but some of hers as well."

Caroline Kennedy   John Kennedy

© 1996 by Caroline B. Kennedy, John F. Kennedy, Jr., and The Estate of Jacqueline Kennedy Onassis

The Complete Auction

Jacqueline Kennedy Onassis's estate consisted of over 5,000 objects, divided into 1,302 lots. The auction was held over a four-day period.

TUESDAY, APRIL 23RD, 7:30 P.M., SESSION 1:
Lots 1-57 (Historical session including furniture, decorations, fine arts, antiquities, books)

WEDNESDAY, APRIL 24TH, 10:00 A.M., SESSION 2:
Lots 58-218 (European furniture, decorations, 19th-century paintings, drawings and prints, books)

WEDNESDAY, APRIL 24TH, 2:00 P.M., SESSION 3:
Lots 219-358 (Furniture, decorations, fine arts)

WEDNESDAY, APRIL 24TH, 6:00 P.M., SESSION 4:
Lots 359-453 (Fine jewelry)

THURSDAY, APRIL 25TH, 10:00 A.M., SESSION 5:
Lots 454-559 (Fashion jewelry)

THURSDAY, APRIL 25TH, 2:00 P.M., SESSION 6:
Lots 560-710 (Decorations, antiquites, Indian miniatures, books)

THURSDAY, APRIL 25TH, 6:00 P.M., SESSION 7:
Lots 711-817 (Sporting art and memorabilia, American paintings and prints, books and manuscripts)

FRIDAY, APRIL 26TH, 10:00 A.M., SESSION 8:
Lots 818-1021 (Fine arts, furniture, decorations, books)

FRIDAY, APRIL 26TH, 2:00 P.M., SESSION 9:
Lots 1022-1195 (Furniture, decorations, fine arts, books, works by Shikler, rocking chair, car)

What follows is a complete summary of all of the lots sold at the auction from least expensive to most expensive. The price each lot sold for includes its buyer's premium. Three lots were withdrawn from the auction. Asterisks denote lots composed of objects that were used either in the Kennedy's Georgetown residence or in the White House.

OBJECT	ESTIMATE	PRICE
Asia, group of six volumes	100–150	1,437
Henri Alain-Fournier, *Le Grand Meaulnes*	300–50	1,725
Unless the Grain Die: Texts by Saint Augustine of Hippo and Saint Ignatius of Antioch	200–400	1,955
Alistair Horne, *Harold Macmillan*, Volume I	200–300	1,955
Print of Washington, D.C.	20–30	2,070
Poetry, group of three volumes	250–350	2,070
Art and art appreciation, group of fourteen volumes	400–600	2,185
Miguel de Andrea, *Pensamiento Cristiano Democrático de Monsen* volumes	300–500	2,300
Michael Flanagan, *Buffalo City*	600–800	2,300
Two decorative botanical pictures	25–35	2,300
Asian art, group of twenty-one illustrated volumes	1,000–1,500	2,300
Auguste Rodin, five reproductions of watercolors	300–500	2,300
19th-century art, group of eleven illustrated volumes	400–600	2,300
Pierce Egan, *Life in London, or, the Day and Night Scenes of Jerry Hawthorn*	300–500	2,300
India, group of eleven volumes	600–900	2,300
Wedgwood oval sauce tureen	50–75	2,300
Literary biography, three works in five volumes	600–800	2,530
Latin and South America, group of eight volumes	500–700	2,530
Austin Henry Layard, *The Monuments of Ninevah*	600–800	2,587
Middle Eastern art, group of fourteen illustrated volumes	300–500	2,587
Photography, group of five volumes	400–600	2,587
American art, group of twenty-one illustrated volumes	800–1,200	2,587
Indian art, pair of volumes	20–300	2,760
Cambodian silver metal box	100–150	2,875
We, the People: the Story of the United States Capitol	300–400	2,875
Biography and literature, pair of volumes inscribed by Father Joseph Leonard	300–500	2,875
Naguib Mahfouz, two volumes, inscribed by the author	200–300	2,875
Group of seventeen volumes on religion and philosophy	500–700	2,875
Two reproductions of botanical prints	25–35	2,875
A. V. Williams Jackson, *A History of India*	400–600	2,875
The ancient world, group of nine volumes	400–600	2,875
Wrightsman Collection, five volumes	400–600	2,875
Poetry and prose, group of seven volumes	600–800	2,875
France, group of four volumes	150–200	2,875
British and Irish art, group of sixteen volumes	300–500	2,875
Jean Théodore Descourtilz, *Pageantry of Brazilian Birds*	200–300	2,875
Charles Louis de Secondat Montesquieu, *Arsace et Isménie, histoire orientale*	200–300	2,875
American glazed redware jar	250–350	2,875
English creamware jelly mold	75–100	2,875
Colorless glass oil lamp, fitted for electricity	80–120	2,875
Supreme Court brief on civil rights and school desegregation	800–1,200	2,990
Fanny Parks, two volumes with forty-nine lithographed plates	300–400	3,162
American art and artists, group of six volumes	400–600	3,162
History and biography, group of six volumes	200–400	3,162
William Manchester, *The Glory and The Dream*	300–500	3,162
France and French culture, pair of volumes	250–350	3,162
J. F. Brennan, *The Evolution of Everyman (Ancestral Lineage of John F. Kennedy)*	200–300	3,162
Super-8 video camera and Polaroid camera	50–80	3,162
W. A. Propert, *The Russian Ballet in Western Europe*	400–600	3,162
Earl Smith, *The Fourth Floor: An Account of the Castro Communist Revolution*	600–800	3,162
George Brookshaw, *A New Treatise on Flower Painting, or, Every Lady Her Own Drawing Master*	400–600	3,162
Abelard and Heloise, *Lettres d'Héloise et d'Abaillard*	600–800	3,162
Art and architecture, group of twenty-two volumes	350–500	3,162
Painted Neolithic jar	300–350	3,220
Metal cup	75–100	3,450
Eric Sloane, *Remember America*, inscribed "To the J. K. O. Library, with infinite admiration. Eric Sloane, 1984"	300–500	3,450
Two volumes about Russia	700–1,000	3,450

Item	Estimate	Sold
In The Russian Style, edited by Jackie Onassis	400–600	3,450
Artist unknown, *Another Song*	100–150	3,450
Four 45-rpm records: Jimmy Dean, *PT-109*, and Frank Sinatra, *High Hopes*	60–80	3,450
Indian art, history, and culture, group of thirty-six volumes	700–1,000	3,450
Indian art, group of twenty-nine volumes	700–1,000	3,450
India, group of seventeen volumes	500–700	3,450
Russian art and history, group of fifteen volumes	300–500	3,450
The presidential years, group of three volumes	200–300	3,450
The Paul Mellon Collection, four volumes	300–500	3,450
Gardens, garden history, and botanical illustration, group of sixteen volumes	400–600	3,450
French chateaux and monuments, group of fifteen volumes	200–300	3,450
Architecture, group of twelve volumes	200–300	3,450
English history and biography, group of twenty-six volumes	300–500	3,450
Middle East, group of twenty-one volumes	200–300	3,450
Eastern literature and poetry, group of twenty-one volumes	150–250	3,450
Modern literature and poetry, group of twenty volumes	150–250	3,450
American history, group of thirty-one volumes	500–700	3,450
Auchincloss family, group of four volumes	100–200	3,450
Staffordshire child's mug, circa 1850	10–150	3,450
Two Chinese porcelain dishes and pair of saucers	100–200	3,450
Pottery lettuce-leaf salad bowl	150–200	3,450
Pair of pottery cabbage-leaf bowls	100–150	3,450
Set of seven lettuce-leaf small dishes	75–100	3,450
Set of nine French terra-cotta cocottes and covers	100–150	3,450
Set of six French stoneware butter pots	75–100	3,450
Milk-glass vase, mounted as an oil lamp and fitted for electricity	75–100	3,450
Group of eight Chinese and Japanese porcelain dishes	400–600	3,450
Philippe Julian, *14, rue du Centre, Neuilly-sur-Seine.*	300–500	3,450
Two Wedgwood diamond-shaped dishes	150–250	3,450
Wedgwood vegetable dish and six soup plates	350–500	3,450
Edward W. West, *Diary of the Late Rajah of Kolhapoor during His Visit to Europe in 1870*	400–600	3,737
The Arts, group of eight volumes	200–400	3,737
Chinese painting, six volumes	400–600	3,737
Recueil d'estampes representant les differents evénemens de la guerre qui a procuré l'indépendance aux Etats Unis de l'Amérique	300–500	3,737
John F. Kennedy, group of fourteen volumes	250–350	3,737
Travel, group of four volumes	300–500	3,737
Pair of Wedgwood oval dishes	100–150	3,737
Pair of Wedgwood oval stands	300–400	3,737
Four 45-rpm records: Jimmy Dean, *PT-109*	80–100	3,910
19th-century Chinese porcelain peach vase	400–600	4,025
Three Georgian teaspoons	150–200	4,025
Group of metal flower holders	150–250	4,025
Alexander Lieberman, *Greece: Gods and Art*	400–600	4,025
European school, *Portrait of a Young Boy*	150–200	4,025
Renaissance art, group of twenty-five illustrated volumes	1,200–1,800	4,025
Art history, Spanish and Dutch, group of nine books	800–1,200	4,025
Loeb Classical Library, group of six volumes	400–600	4,025
Jean Cocteau, autographed note	150–200	4,025
Biography, group of thirty-four volumes	300–500	4,025
J. L. Adolphus, *Memoirs of Queen Caroline*, two volumes	400–600	4,025
Paris and its environs, group of nine volumes	7000–1,000	4,025
School of Paris, group of eleven volumes	400–600	4,025
Country houses and villas, group of twelve volumes	300–500	4,025
French history and biography, group of thirty-six volumes	500–700	4,025
Literature, group of twenty-six volumes by American and English authors	200–300	4,025
contemporary American and English women, group of thirty-seven volumes	250–350	4,025
Staffordshire mug, circa 1840	100–150	4,025
Three Chinese porcelain bowls and a dish	400–600	4,025
Nine Chinese porcelain blue and white small dishes	75–100	4,025
Pair of pottery commemorative mugs, inscribed "USS *Joseph P. Kennedy, Jr.*"	100–150	4,025
Pair of pottery commemorative mugs, inscribed "USS *Joseph P. Kennedy, Jr.*"	100–150	4,025
Four circular rattan garden seats	75–100	4,025
19th-century cut silhouette picture of a man	200–400	4,025
Blue and white porcelain waste bowl	150–250	4,025
Robert Werlich, *Beast Butler*, with copy of *Profiles in Courage*	300–500	4,025
Sheldon and Wilmarth Lewis, *One Man's Education*	200–300	4,025
Thomas Buchanan Read, *Sheridan's Ride*	300–500	4,025
John F. Kennedy, group of fifteen volumes	250–350	4,025
Susan Barron and John Cage, *Another Song*	800–1,200	4,025
John Emmet Hughes, *The Ordeal of Power: A Political Memoir of the Eisenhower Years*	300–500	4,025
History and biography, group of seventeen volumes	200–300	4,025
Pair of Wedgwood oval stands	400–600	4,025
Reproduction of painting of a woman lying in a bed	25–50	4,255

Item	Estimate	Sold
American school pencil drawing, *Woman Riding a Horse*	150–200	4,312
Michele, *Patiently Waiting*, reproduction with hand coloring	50–75	4,312
The ancient world, group of thirty-two volumes	300–500	4,312
Mediterranean and Near East, group of eight volumes	400–600	4,312
Oriental art, group of ten volumes	600–900	4,312
Biography, group of three volumes	150–200	4,312
John F. Kennedy, group of twelve volumes	250–350	4,312
John F. Kennedy, group of twelve volumes	250–350	4,312
Dr. Benjamin Spock, *The Common Sense of Baby and Child Care*	150–250	4,312
Biography, group of three volumes	500–700	4,312
Set of twelve Wedgwood dinner plates	700–1,000	4,312
Pair of stoneware vases mounted as lamps	600–900	4,312
Silver electroplate water pitcher and two trays	100–150	4,500
Staffordshire earthenware dish and cover	125–175	4,600
Group of brass bowls, metal coasters, and baskets	75–100	4,600
Blue and white Chinese porcelain stacking container and cover	250–350	4,600
Seven 19th-century polychrome plates	500–800	4,600
Three pairs of ivory salt shakers and pepper grinders	150–200	4,600
Ludwig Bemelmans, *On Board Noah's Ark*, inscribed "To Jackie with love, Love Ludwig"	400–600	4,600
Fynes Moryson, first edition of Moryson's travel book with woodcuts	800–1,200	4,600
The John F. Kennedy Memorial at Runnymeade: Dedicatory Remarks, bound and printed	400–600	4,600
Creative America, texts by JFK, James Baldwin, Robert Frost, et al.	400–600	4,600
Oratio Dominica, two volumes	1,500–2,000	4,600
Philip B. Kunhardt, Jr., *Lincoln*, inscribed by author, "For Jackie, Christmas 1992"	300–500	4,600
Jacqueline Duheme, two watercolors	75–125	4,600
Lithograph, *Washington from the President's House*	600–800	4,600
Ink-and-chalk drawing, *A Horse and a Groom*	1,500–2,000	4,600
Michael Flanagan, *Untitled (Desert Station)*	150–200	4,600
Silver trophy goblet	100–150	4,600
Silver trophy goblet	100–150	4,600
Jaipur school, *Portrait of Maharaja Pratap Singh of Jaipur*	500–700	4,600
Illustration from a manuscript of Persian poetry	500–700	4,600
Christian Berard, *Etude*, gouache on paper	1,000–1,500	4,600
Literature, group of seven volumes	800–1,200	4,600
The Times, London, framed article on the sacking of Washington, D.C.	200–300	4,600
Russia, two volumes	800–1,200	4,600
Decorative arts, group of twenty-five volumes	80–1,200	4,600
Gardens and garden history, group of twenty-one volumes	300–500	4,600
Reference, group of twenty-three volumes	400–600	4,600
English country houses, group of twelve volumes	300–500	4,600
French literature, group of forty-seven volumes	500–700	4,600
19th-century English and American poetry, group of nine volumes	300–500	4,600
Modern English and American poetry, group of thirty volumes	200–300	4,600
French biography, group of six volumes	300–500	4,600
19th-century French mug and beaker	125–175	4,600
Three silver-lustre julep cups and porcelain coffee cup with saucer	150–250	4,600
Pair of bone china sugar bowls and a berry dish	75–100	4,600
Five ceramic vessels	100–150	4,600
Pair of pottery commemorative mugs, inscribed "USS *Joseph P. Kennedy, Jr.*"	100–150	4,600
Green-painted wood wall bracket	150–200	4,600
Japanese Imari porcelain bowl	200–300	4,600
Canton porcelain blue and white bowl	125–175	4,600
Set of four Japanese Imari porcelain dishes	200–300	4,600
Paris porcelain saucer and three English porcelain saucers	150–250	4,600
Two Staffordshire porcelain teabowls and three saucers	150–250	4,600
Pierre Dupuy, *Histoire des plus illustres favoris ancient et moderns*	400–600	4,600
Children's books on JFK, group of nine volumes	200–300	4,600
Children's books on JFK, group of thirteen volumes,	250–350	4,600
John F. Kennedy, group of twenty volumes	300–500	4,600
John F. Kennedy, group of twelve volumes	250–350	4,600
John F. Kennedy, group of eleven volumes	250–350	4,600
English culture, group of seven volumes	300–500	4,600
English literature, group of twelve volumes	300–500	4,600
Theater, group of four volumes	300–500	4,600
Poetry, group of four volumes	600–800	4,600
English porcelain scalloped dish	150–250	4,600
Pink-glass boudoir lamp	200–300	4,600
Two dark green side chairs	200–300	4,600
Silver trophy goblet	100–150	4,830
Pierluigi Caterina, *Omaggio a Jacqueline Kennedy*, watercolor	250–300	4,887
Modern photography, group of four volumes	500–800	4,887
India, group of three volumes	100–200	4,887
JFK and Ireland, group of five volumes	400–600	4,887
Biography, group of six volumes	800–1,200	4,887
Biography, group of seven volumes	1,000–1,500	4,887

Item	Estimate	Price
John F. Kennedy, *The Burden and the Glory*, group of twenty copies	400–600	4,887
Richard M. Hunt, *Designs for the Gateways of the Southern Entrances to the Central Park*	500–700	4,887
Foreign affairs and politics, group of four volumes	700–1,000	4,887
Travel, group of eighteen volumes	300–500	4,887
Pair of Wedgwood diamond-shaped dishes	150–250	4,887
Coalport pair of plates	200–300	5,175
Chinese porcelain teapot stand	200–300	5,175
Ivory and tortoiseshell gourd container and a pair of tusk-section bracelets	150–200	5,175
Pair of electrogilt wine coasters	50–100	5,175
Group of electroplate flatware, including martini stirrers, sauce ladle, egg slicer, and carving knife	100–150	5,175
Four pairs of ivory salt shakers and pepper grinders	200–300	5,175
Six volumes on decorative arts	400–600	5,175
Sir John Pope-Hennessy, group of four volumes signed, "To Jackie, with every Affectionate wish from John, 14.iv.1994"	800–1,200	5,175
A. L. Rowse, *Homosexuals in History*	600–800	5,175
Group of six volumes about modern history	500–800	5,175
Robert Lowell, five presentation copies of various volumes, inscribed by the author	1,200–1,800	5,175
Group of five volumes on advertising and publishing, each inscribed from the author	600–900	5,175
Canton porcelain, "Famille-Rose" soup plate	50–75	5,175
Louis XVI giltwood-frame mirror	400–600	5,175
Gilt-metal belt	250–350	5,175
Miscellaneous group of jewelry, including beads and pendant	150–200	5,175
Silkwork picture	400–600	5,175
Greek icon triptych	1,200–1,500	5,175
Silver trophy goblet	100–150	5,175
Silver trophy goblet	100–150	5,175
Silver trophy goblet	100–150	5,175
Warrior on Horseback, Deccan, 18th/19th century	500–700	5,175
Jacqueline Bouvier Kennedy, *One Special Summer*	100–150	5,175
World War I, group of five volumes	600–800	5,175
Three volumes on the Congress of the United States	800–1,200	5,175
John F. Kennedy, group of twenty-two volumes by or about the president	800–1,200	5,175
The White House library list, four volumes	500–700	5,175
British biography, three volumes	600–800	5,175
American politics, group of nine volumes	800–1,200	5,175
Horses and horsemanship, group of nine volumes	400–600	5,175
Biography, group of fifty volumes of journals, diaries and letters	300–500	5,175
Pair of Italian ashtrays and modern oyster plate	50–75	5,175
Four Japanese Imari porcelain scalloped circular dishes	300–400	5,175
Children's books on JFK, group of ten volumes	200–300	5,175
Children's books on JFK, group of eight volumes	200–300	5,175
John F. Kennedy, group of twelve volumes	250–350	5,175
New York City, group of four volumes	200–300	5,175
French history, group of six volumes	300–500	5,175
Russia, group of eight volumes	200–300	5,175
Russian literature, group of ten volumes	300–500	5,175
Jacqueline Kennedy Onassis, group of twenty-three volumes by or edited by Jackie	300–500	5,175
Pair of Wedgwood creamware cress dishes	300–400	5,175
22-karat gold and enamel Byzantine-style icon roundel	700–900	5,462
Antiquity: Egyptian, Greek, Roman and early Byzantine art, forty-four volumes	1,000–1,500	5,462
John F. Kennedy, group of twenty-five volumes	500–700	5,462
Michel Beurdeley, *Chinese Trade Porcelain*	150–250	5,462
John F. Kennedy, group of fifteen volumes by or about the president	400–600	5,462
Dark-green-painted stool	50–75	5,462
Coalport pair of dessert plates	200–300	5,750
Blue and white Chinese porcelain trays	250–350	5,750
19th-century Chinese porcelain bowl	250–350	5,750
19th-century painted papier-mâché tray	80–120	5,750
Set of eight French gold-plated beakers	400–600	5,750
Four pairs of ivory salt shakers and pepper grinders	200–300	5,750
Two pairs of ivory salt shaker and pepper grinders and six pepper grinders	250–350	5,750
J. C. Holt, *Magna Carta*	1,000–1,500	5,750
John Betjeman, *Summoned by Bells*, inscribed by the author	400–600	5,750
Miguel de Cervantes Saavedra, *The History and Adventures of the Renowned Don Quixote*	250–350	5,750
Group of three volumes on health, each inscribed from the author	300–500	5,750
Group of five devotional texts, inscribed by Father Joseph Leonard	800–1,200	5,750
Pair of china soup plates, "Famille-Rose"	200–300	5,750
Louis XVI-style giltwood frame mounted as mirror	600–800	5,750
Silver belt	400–600	5,750
Coral and mother-of-pearl brooch	200–300	5,750
Gilt-metal and simulated coral bead necklace and simulated ear clips	400–500	5,750
Walt Kuhn, *Clown, Woman, Horse*, pen and ink	800–1,200	5,750
Silver trophy goblet	100–150	5,750
19th-century architectural study of a lake pavilion	700–1,000	5,750
Garhwal school, *A Lady Playing with a Peacock on a Terrace*	1,500–2,500	5,750
Joseph Alsop, *From the Silent Earth: A Report on the Greek Bronze Age*	500–800	5,750
Art and art appreciation, group of five volumes	200–400	5,750
Carved and painted wood half-hull model of the *Wianno, Sr.*	800–1,200	5,750
Framed wedding announcement, Grover Cleveland	200–300	5,750
European politics and policy, group of three volumes	800–1,200	5,750
European politics and policy, group of three volumes	800–1,200	5,750
American literature, group of four volumes	800–1,200	5,750
Literature: anthologies and criticism, four volumes	600–800	5,750
Fine and decorative arts, group of 105 volumes	400–500	5,750
Interior design, group of fifteen volumes	300–500	5,750
Versailles, group of twenty-one volumes	500–700	5,750
Horses and sporting art, group of seven illustrated volumes	200–300	5,750
Greek and Roman literature, group of fifteen volumes	300–500	5,750
Literature, group of seven volumes of fiction, poetry, and nonfiction	300–500	5,750
Four English porcelain tea and coffee wares	125–175	5,750
English porcelain coffee cup, three saucers, and three saucer dishes	75–100	5,750
Set of five French porcelain "Man in Space" plates	200–300	5,750
Porcelain commemorative cabinet plate inscribed to the First Lady	100–150	5,750
Bamboo armchair, early 19th century	250–450	5,750
Chinese Ying Qing bowl, Yuan dynasty	400–600	5,750
Children's books on JFK, group of thirteen volumes	250–350	5,750
Mexico, group of six volumes	300–500	5,750
Kennedy family, group of nine volumes on history of the family	200–300	5,750
Women and women authors, group of nine volumes	500–700	5,750
Architecture and landscape design, group of twelve volumes	400–600	5,750
The Houghton Shahnameh, two volumes	1,500–2,000	5,750
Pair of Wedgwood creamware basins	300–500	5,750
English reticulated oval basket and egg cups	200–300	5,750
Pair of Japanese porcelain bowls	100–150	5,750
Chinese garden seat, mounted as a lamp	600–900	5,750
American maple wall mirror	75–100	5,750
19th-century Neapolitan school, *Mt. Vesuvius*	1,000–1,500	5,750
Angela Piotrowska Wittman, *Ornament with Blue S hell-Shaped Flowers*, watercolor	200–300	5,750
Travel in Africa, Asia, and the Middle East, group of twenty-seven volumes	300–500	5,865
18th-century Indian painting, *Two Ladies in Discussion on a Palace Terrace*	1,500–2,500	6,037
Photography, group of twenty-one volumes	400–600	6,037
Jacqueline Kennedy Onassis, *Portrait of a Young Woman*	200–300	6,325
Red and White Flowers, oil on glass	300–500	6,325
Chinese porcelain bowl and jars with covers	300–500	6,325
Chinese porcelain green reticulated oval stand	100–150	6,325
Four volumes on decorative arts	500–700	6,325
Joe McCarthy, *The Remarkable Kennedys*, with presidential bookplate	600–800	6,325
Randolph Churchill, *Lord Derby: King of Lancashire*, with presidential bookplate	400–600	6,325
Artist unknown, *Portrait of JFK*	50–75	6,325
Georges Rouault, *Misere*	600–800	6,325
Jan de Bisschop (1628–1671), *Soldiers in an Encampment*	4,000–6,000	6,325
18th-century French school, *Profile Portrait of a Lady*	300–500	6,325
Louis XV-style painted mirror	800–1,000	6,325
Louis XV-style button-tufted tabouret	800–1,000	6,325
19th-century cane-seat side chair	200–300	6,325
Gilt-metal pectoral and silver-gilt armlet	250–350	6,325
Four silver pendants and three metal bead necklaces	350–450	6,325
Simulated pearl and emerald brooch	250–350	6,325
Simulated diamond and jet brooch and two pairs of ear clips	300–400	6,325
Gilt-metal basketweave holder	20–40	6,325
Two brass tobacco boxes	80–120	6,325
19th-century pine milking stool	80–120	6,325
Three electroplate salt cellars	50–80	6,325
Painted ivory in leather case, *Princely Couple on a Terrace*, Delhi	2,500–3,500	6,325
13th-century Persian lusterware cup	400–600	6,325
The Military Costume of Turkey	800–1,200	6,325
Fashion, costume, jewelry and style, forty volumes	800–1,200	6,325
American architecture, group of nineteen volumes	400–600	6,325
Fiction, group of eight volumes	300–500	6,325
James Seymour, *A Racehorse with Jockey Up*	800–1,200	6,325
Philosophy and religion, six volumes	1,000–1,500	6,325
White House guides, group of various editions	300–500	6,325
Modern literature, group of thirty-seven volumes	500–700	6,325
Group of thirty volumes edited by Jacqueline Kennedy Onassis	500–700	6,325
Manuel Toussaint, *La Catedral de Mexico y el Sagrario Metropolitano*	300–500	6,325
Ballets Russes, collection of illustrations	1,500–2,500	6,325
Russia, group of nineteen volumes	300–500	6,325

Set of eight Derby porcelain dessert plates	100–150	6,325
Chinese porcelain shell-shaped dish	150–250	6,325
Chines porcelain oval dish	150–250	6,325
Chinese porcelain soap dish, cover, and liner	200–300	6,325
Wooden oak box, small mahogany box, pair of opera glasses, small bell, and tinware candlestick	500–700	6,325
American biography, group of five volumes	300–500	6,325
John F. Kennedy, group of nineteen volumes	300–500	6,325
Robert F. Kennedy, group of twenty-three volumes	400–600	6,325
Women authors, group of eight volumes	600–800	6,325
White House guides, group of various editions	75–100	6,325
Jacqueline Kennedy Onassis, group of twenty-eight volumes by or edited by Jackie	400–600	6,325
China, two engraved maps	200–400	6,325
Set of six Wedgwood dessert plates	250–350	6,325
Tibetan turquoise and silver amulet box	200–300	6,325
Modern painters, group of five volumes	300–500	6,612
Hand-colored seashell engravings	700–800	6,612
Coalport set of eleven plates	500–700	6,900
Chinese porcelain spoon tray	100–150	6,900
Chinese porcelain spoon tray and berry dish	100–150	6,900
Chinese porcelain saucer	150–200	6,900
Set of twelve Davenport soup plates and ten dinner plates	800–1,200	6,900
Set of seven Bing and Grondahl teacups and nine saucers	75–100	6,900
Blue and white Chinese porcelain jardinières	400–600	6,900
Blue and white Chinese porcelain vessels	500–700	6,900
Silver sugar caster	60–100	6,900
Set of five Cambodian silver finger bowls	400–600	6,900
Silver-plated silent butler engraved with the initials "JLB"	200–400	6,900
Group of silver flatware, including iced tea spoons, sugar tongs, and nut crackers	300–500	6,900
Abba Ebban, *Heritage: Civilization and the Jews*, inscribed to Jackie from the author	400–600	6,900
Truman Capote, selected writings, inscribed "For Jackie with Truman's admiration and affection, 5 June 1963"	600–800	6,900
19th-century French school watercolor, *Garden Façade of a Chateau*	800–1,000	6,900
Rochus Van Veen (died 1709), *Duck*	600–800	6,900
Louis XVI-style gray painted marble-top table	400–600	6,900
Three multicolor bead necklaces	300–400	6,900
Group of Bedouin jewelry	400–600	6,900
Group of four bead necklaces	200–250	6,900
Gilt-metal and white bead necklace	200–300	6,900
Three metal chain necklaces	250–350	6,900
Set of ten porcelain cups and twelve saucers	50–75	6,900
Two prints, *Banque de France* and *Timbre Royal*	50–75	6,900
Pair of silver-gilt salt cellars	500–700	6,900
Electroplate vegetable dish with covers	50–100	6,900
18th-century Indian painting, *Princess Entertained by Two Female Musicians*	2,000–3,000	6,900
19th-century Mughal, *A Gentleman Celebrating Holi with Five Ladies*	1,000–1,500	6,900
13th-century Thai clay votive tablet	500–700	6,900
Philomé Obin, *Paradise Terrestre Après Je Péché*	5,000–7,000	6,900
Préfète Duffaut, *Sans titre*	800–1,200	6,900
Indian philosophy and culture, group of ten volumes	400–600	6,900
Art exhibitions and collections, group of seventeen volumes	500–700	6,900
Modern artists, group of four volumes	300–500	6,900
Russian art and style, group of twenty-nine volumes	300–500	6,900
Ballet, dance, and theater, group of twenty-three volumes	400–600	6,900
Arthur S. Link, *Wilson: The Road to the White House*	1,200–1,800	6,900
James Seymour, *The Gallop to the Right Hand*	800–1,200	6,900
The Cambridge Modern History, eleven volumes	1,000–1,500	6,900
Modern warfare and armament, group of four volumes	1,500–2,500	6,900
Sports, group of six volumes	500–800	6,900
The White House, group of twelve volumes	800–1,200	6,900
The White House, group of six volumes	200–300	6,900
The Kennedy White House Parties and spiral-bound book of photos	400–600	6,900
Fox-hunting, group of six volumes	500–800	6,900
John F. Kennedy, Inaugural Address phonographic album	100–200	6,900
White House and presidency, group of fifty volumes	300–500	6,900
William Manchester, *One Brief Shining Moment*	200–400	6,900
Alfred Brittain, et al., *Women in All Ages and in All Countries*, eight volumes	300–500	6,900
White House guides, group of various editions	300–500	6,900
Staffordshire candlestick, circa 1820	150–250	6,900
Staffordshire figure of whippet	150–250	6,900
Glazed pottery, "Lettuce Leaf," part service	600–900	6,900
Pair of barley-twist oak candlesticks	200–300	6,900
Three hand-colored engravings	200–300	6,900
Porcelain saucer dish, circa 1800	100–150	6,900
Chinese porcelain cylindrical jar and cover	200–300	6,900
Sterling Mulbry, *The Corner of Louisiana (for Walker Percy)*	700–900	6,900
French literature, group of thirteen volumes	800–1,200	6,900
Greek literature, group of six volumes	500–800	6,900
Noel Coward, *Present Indicative*	200–300	6,900
Jacqueline Kennedy Onassis, group of twenty volumes about the Bouvier family or Mrs. Onassis, some with forwards by her	400–600	6,900
Poetry, group of twelve volumes	600–800	6,900
English literature, group of fifteen volumes	500–700	6,900
Women's biography, group of seven volumes	500–700	6,900
French style and design, group of eight volumes	400–600	6,900
Literature, group of eighteen volumes	300–500	6,900
Set of twelve Wedgwood dinner plates	800–1,200	6,900
Chinese porcelain snuff bottle	100–150	6,900
Photograph of an Aaron Shikler portrait	50–75	7,187
Hand-colored seashell engravings	700–800	7,475
19th-century Regency dressing mirror	1,200–1,500	7,475
Chinese jadeite and enamel-mounted silver hand mirror	600–800	7,475
19th-century brass and wrought-iron standing trivet	500–700	7,475
White House guides, group of various editions	300–500	7,475
Rogers Turner, *Still Life with Tulips in a Chinese Vase and Pears on a Ledge*	800–1,200	7,475
Louis XVI style white-painted upholstered stool	500–700	7,475
18th-century marble-top low table	1,500–2,500	7,475
Chanel, pair of gilt-metal simulated pearl button ear clips	200–300	7,475
Two simulated ivory bead necklaces and simulated ivory ear clips	400–500	7,475
Group of five necklaces	250–350	7,475
Three pairs of gilt-metal ear clips	300–400	7,475
Simulated diamond bangle bracelet and two pairs of ear clips	200–300	7,475
Silver buckle belt and simulated diamond and ruby buckle belt	400–500	7,475
Two simulated colored stone pendants	250–350	7,475
Three simulated gem set chains	150–250	7,475
Five silver-mounted cut-glass flasks	150–200	7,475
15th-century illustrated folio from manuscript of the *Khamsa*	2,500–3,500	7,475
18th-century Mewar school, *Portrait of a Stallion with His Groom*	1,500–2,000	7,475
4th-century B.C. Greek terra-cotta figure of Dionysos	3,000–5,000	7,475
Art history and appreciation, group of ten volumes	400–600	7,475
James Seymour, *A Groom Watering a Horse at Trough*	800–1,200	7,475
19th-century American school, *Calligraphic Specimen Picture of a Bird*	200–400	7,475
19th-century engraved scrimshaw whalebone busk	700–900	7,475
Louis Antoine Fauvelet de Bourrienne, *Memoirs of Napoleon Bonaparte*	400–600	7,475
The White House and the presidency, group of sixteen volumes	300–500	7,475
Illustrated and bound copy of JFK's French speeches	600–800	7,475
American politics, group of six volumes	400–600	7,475
Alois Podhajsky, *Die Spanische Hofreitschule*	300–500	7,475
Pair of English enameled teabowls, circa 1775	75–100	7,475
Two lithographs, *Henry Clay* and *John Marshall*	100–150	7,475
Children's books on JFK, group of eighteen volumes	300–500	7,475
French literature, group of twelve volumes	500–700	7,475
Literature and criticism, group of eleven volumes	400–600	7,475
History and politics, group of twenty volumes	400–600	7,475
Children's literature, group of fourteen titles	150–250	7,475
Travel: Europe and the Americas, group of thirty-three volumes	700–1,000	7,475
History and biography, group of twenty-nine volumes	600–800	7,475
Wedgwood creamware covered butter tubs	300–500	7,475
Staffordshire cruet stand and ewers	200–300	7,475
Andy Warhol, *Mao Dead*, autographed copy of the *New York Post*	200–300	7,762
Coalport salad bowl	300–500	8,050
Derby porcelain coffee service	600–900	8,050
Pair of Chinese school 19th-century watercolors	400–600	8,050
Blue and white Chinese porcelain garden seats	1,200–1,800	8,050
Empire-style bronze hand mirror	500–700	8,050
Four Indian electroplate tumblers	100–150	8,050
Set of eight "Nantucket" dessert plates	200–300	8,050
Oak fragment from London Bridge inscribed "to Janet Lee (Bouvier)..."	400–600	8,050
English electroplate salver engraved in center "JLB"	80–120	8,050
Pair of blue marbleized-wood lamps	300–500	8,050
Winter antiques show catalog, 1962	500–700	8,050
White House guides, group of various editions	300–500	8,050
Jacqueline Bouvier Kennedy, Portrait of a Valiant Lady and *Kennedy in Germany*, phonograph albums	200–400	8,050
16th-century Florentine school, *A Young Boy Standing in a Niche*	1,000–1,500	8,050
18th-century Italian school, *Study of a Young Man in a Hat and Cloak*	1,500–2,000	8,050
Henry Singleton (1766–1839), *Portrait of a Young Girl, Said to Be Miss Simpson*	500–700	8,050
18th-century Venetian school, *Studies of Figures in Procession*, drawing	1,500–2,000	8,050
Pair of Louis XVI-style cane-backed painted chairs	1,500–2,000	8,050
Two hinged bangle bracelets	300–400	8,050
Gilt-metal and simulated diamond necklace and pair of dress clips	200–300	8,050
Gilt-metal and simulated colored stone chain necklace, Chanel	400–600	8,050

Item	Estimate	Lot
French silver toothbrush box and cover	120–180	8,050
Set of four gilt-metal flasks in leather case	50–100	8,050
Russian silver-gilt bonbonnière	700–900	8,050
Russian silver-gilt vodka cup	500–700	8,050
Pair of silver salt cellars and electroplate pepperettes	80–120	8,050
Costume and fashion, group of nine volumes	600–800	8,050
French decorative arts, group of seventeen volumes	800–1,200	8,050
Group of eleven Kennedy half dollars	200–300	8,050
Abraham Lincoln, group of seven volumes	300–500	8,050
American history, group of ten volumes	500–700	8,050
American politics and policy, group of four volumes	1,000–1,500	8,050
Larry Vrzalik and Michael Minor, *From the President's Pen: An Illustrated Guide To Presidential Autographs*	600–800	8,050
Biography, group of eight volumes	400–600	8,050
Pair of Staffordshire whippet inkwells	300–400	8,050
French ormolu candlestick, fitted for electricity	200–300	8,050
Pair of watercolors of flowers, Cantonese school, 19th century	1,000–1,500	8,050
Reeve Schley, *Dunes*, watercolor on paper	800–1,200	8,050
Mary Faulconer, *Birds, Eggs and Grasses*	2000–400	8,050
French literature, group of eleven volumes	1,000–1,500	8,050
French literature, group of ten volumes	400–600	8,050
American literature, group of fourteen volumes	600–800	8,050
Literature and criticism, group of five volumes	500–700	8,050
Hawaii, two items	300–500	8,050
Coalport sauce tureens, covers, and stands	600–800	8,625
Chinese cloisonné enamel bird-form box	125–175	8,625
English silver-gilt bowl	800–1,200	8,625
19th-century steel and brass trivet	400–600	8,625
White House guides, group of various editions	300–500	8,625
Group of eighteen volumes on Eastern religion and thought	500–700	8,625
Set of three lithographs of scenic landscapes	100–150	8,625
Jean-Baptiste Oudry (1686–1755), *Study of a Spaniel Barking*	2,000–3,000	8,625
P.H., *Study of an Owl on a Stump*	700–900	8,625
Louis Philippe gilt-bronze dog-form paper clip, with hinged mouth	500–700	8,625
Louis XV upholstered banquette	1,500–2,500	8,625
Louis XVI-style white-upholstered chair	200,300	8,625
Fruitwood table *vide poche*	300–500	8,625
Group of silver and hardstone jewelry, including chains, ear clips	600–800	8,625
Pair of simulated pearl and diamond ear clips and two pendants	250–350	8,625
Caucasian silver and niello belt	500–700	8,625
British watercolor and ink, *Gentleman on Horseback by a Gothic Folly*	200–300	8,625
Modern photography	400–600	8,625
Art history, group of forty-nine volumes	600–800	8,625
Circle of Carle Vernet, *A Groom Mounted on a Horse in a Landscape*	700–1,000	8,625
Group of thirty lapel pins representing various countries	200–300	8,625
Biographies of women, group of forty-three volumes	700–1,000	8,625
Pair of Chinese porcelain plates	150–250	8,625
Pair of Chinese porcelain quatrefoil dishes	100–150	8,625
Greek icon of the Deesis, 19th century	1,200–1,800	8,625
Two lithographs, *Andrew Jackson* and *John Randolph*	100–150	8,625
Two Chinese porcelain brush pots and rectangular tray	400–600	8,625
White House guides, group of various editions	300–500	8,625
American women, group of eighteen volumes	700–1,000	8,625
Five English table articles	250–350	8,625
Royal Worcester bone china dinner and coffee service	400–600	8,625
Set of nine Chinese dinner plates	1,200–1,800	8,625
Victorian paint-decorated etagère	1,200–1,500	8,625
Two yellow metal necklaces and a pair of ear clips	100–150	8,625
White House Library: A Short-Title List	1,500–2,500	9,200
Collection of woven baskets	150–200	9,200
Japanese black-lacquered cabinet	1,500–2,500	9,200
Blue and white Dutch Delft flower bricks	50–75	9,200
Silver caster engraved with the initial "K"	100–150	9,200
*Pair of electroplate wine coasters	200–400	9,200
Twelve Grosvenor bone china dinner plates	400–600	9,200
Silver platter engraved in center "JLB"	250–350	9,200
Five pairs of ivory salt shakers and pepper grinders	250–350	9,200
Jacqueline and Lee Bouvier, *One Special Summer*	100–150	9,200
Robert Berk, *John F. Kennedy: A Portrait Bust*	500–1,000	9,200
Eugene Berman, *The Columns of Nathor*, signed and dated 1964	800–1,200	9,200
Porcelain jardinière, circa 1810	500–700	9,200
*Chinese porcelain oval sugar bowl and cover, teapot stand, and spoon tray	300–500	9,200
Louis XVI-style upholstered tabouret	1,500–2,000	9,200
Group of five bead necklaces	400–600	9,200
Group of four choker necklaces	150–200	9,200
Kangra school, *Two Women Celebrating the Festival of Holi on a Palace Terrace*	3,000–5,000	9,200
South Indian reverse glass painting, 19th-century	300–500	9,200
Horses and horsemanship, group of four volumes	300–500	9,200
Staffordshire equestrian group of the "Empress of France"	150–250	9,200
Pair of George III–style mahogany side chairs	400–600	9,200
Maple and ash child's writing armchair	200–300	9,200
Chinese porcelain bowl, circa 1750	500–700	9,200
Pericle Fazzini (Italian, 1913–87), *Horse and Rider*, bronze sculpture	1,000–1,500	9,200
White House guides, group of various editions	300–500	9,200
Women's biography, group of nine works	700–1,000	9,200
Black-painted three-legged stool	75–125	9,200
Regency rosewood three-tier etagère	500–800	9,200
Yellow-lacquered burlap low table	500–700	9,200
Staffordshire white charger	200–300	9,430
Set of ten porcelain "Soldiers of the American Army" plates	200–300	9,775
Hand-colored lithograph and two hand-colored engravings, *La Grande Cascade de Longchamps*, *Le Parc d'Ermenviole*, and *Vue General d'Ermenviole*	200–300	9,775
Pierre Montani, 19th century, *The French Empress Eugenie Visiting the Baths of the Imperial Palace of Ciragan*	1,200–1,800	9,775
Canton porcelain, late 19th-century breakfast cups and fifteen saucers	1,500–2,500	9,775
19th-century Bessarabian kilim rug	600–800	9,775
Gilt-metal and simulated colored stone choker	300–400	9,775
Two gilt-metal and colored bead station necklaces	100–200	9,775
Two pairs simulated diamond and colored stone ear clips	300–400	9,775
English electroplate berry spoons	40–80	9,775
Silver cigarette lighter	150–200	9,775
1st/2nd-century Roman bronze figure of Aphrodite	4,000–6,000	9,775
716–30 B.C. Egyptian bronze figure of Nefertum	200–300	9,775
Old Master paintings and drawings, thirty-five volumes	1,500–2,000	9,775
Robert M. LaFollette, volume 2	1,000–1,500	9,775
John James Audubon, *Marsh Tern*	1,500–2,000	9,775
Currier and Ives, *American Thoroughbreds*	300–400	9,775
White House guides, group of various editions	300–500	9,775
John F. Kennedy, *A Compilation of Statements and Speeches during His Service in the United States Senate and House of Representatives*	800–1,200	9,775
Memorial tributes to the president, made in the House of Lords	600–800	9,775
Group of twenty-one slides of JFK with viewer	400–600	9,775
Gardens and gardening, group of six books	600–800	9,775
Biography, group of seven volumes	400–600	9,775
Set of five French porcelain "Man in Space" plates	250–350	9,775
Pair of Chinese porcelain plates	125–175	9,775
English literature, group of fourteen volumes	400–600	9,775
American architecture, group of eleven volumes	700–900	9,775
John F. Kennedy, group of twelve volumes by or about the president	500–700	9,775
Meissen porcelain part coffee service	300–400	9,775
Coalport set of twelve plates	900–1,200	10,350
Japanese lacquer brush box	250–350	10,350
Silver three-piece coffee service	450–650	10,350
Set of six Spode "Fox Hunting" dinner plates	200–300	10,350
19th-century desk tray	150–175	10,350
Louis Dupré, hand-colored lithograph, c. 1850	300–500	10,350
Set of six hand-colored engravings of theatrical sets	200–300	10,350
Gaetano de Rosa (1690–1770), *Study of Bull's Head*	500–700	10,350
Simulated pearl and crystal bead tassel necklace	150–250	10,350
Two pairs of gilt-metal ear clips	150–250	10,350
Three gilt bead necklaces and gilt metal ear clips	200–300	10,350
Silk rope and simulated stone necklace and matching ear clips	500–600	10,350
Gilt metal and simulated pearl necklace and simulated diamond ear clips	200–300	10,350
Mehwar school, circa 1760, *Maharana Ari Singh and a Nobleman Hunting Wild Boar*	2,000–3,000	10,350
Sorines Mentor, *Sans titre*	600–800	10,350
19th and 20th-century art, group of thirty-three volumes	800–1,200	10,350
Hand-colored lithograph, *Battle of New Orleans 1815*	300–400	10,350
Frank Dahl, *The Next Democratic Convention: Now Is There Anyone Here Whose Name Isn't John F. Kennedy?*, cartoon drawing	500–700	10,350
American history, group of three volumes	600–800	10,350
Set of eight Royal Worcester dessert plates	300–500	10,350
Russian brass icon triptych	350–600	10,350
Two hand-colored lithographs, circa 1850	100–200	10,350
Raymond Crosby, *The Ball*, pencil on paper	500–700	10,350
Jacques Villon, *Au Concert* and *Study of a Woman*, double-sided drawing	800–1,200	10,350
Washington and the White House, group of seventeen volumes	400–600	10,350
Italy, group of ten volumes	600–800	10,350
Set of five English reticulated plates	200–300	10,350
Chinese porcelain lotus bowl	75–125	10,350
Aaron Shikler, *A Study of Caroline Kennedy*	2,000–3,000	10,350
Louis XVI gilt and tôle *peinte brûle* parfum	500–700	10,350
White-painted bedside table	300–400	10,925
Compton Mackenzie, *On Moral Courage*	2,000–3,000	10,925

Item	Estimate	Price
*Set of two hand-colored engravings of French interiors and window drapery	100–125	10,925
Hand-colored engraving, *View of la Place de Louis XVI et la Salle d'Opera*	200–300	10,925
*18th-century Continental school, *A Hunt Servant with Hooded Hawks on a Portable Perch*	2,000–3,000	10,925
Rochus Van Veen (died 1709), *Study of a Doormouse*	2,000–3,000	10,925
Group of simulated turquoise and mother-of-pearl jewelry	150–250	10,925
Group of animal and insect jewelry	400–500	10,925
Two pairs of gilt-metal ear clips and pendant necklace	300–400	10,925
5th/4th-century B.C. Greek vessel and 2nd/1st-century B.C. red jug	500–800	10,925
Virginia and the South, group of thirty five books and pamphlets	600–800	10,925
French literature, group of six volumes	500–700	10,925
Paris and Versailles, group of twelve volumes	700–1,000	10,925
Jacqueline Kennedy and the White House, pair of paperback editions	100–200	10,925
Photograph of the Kennedys, Johnsons, and Trumans at Eisenhower's funeral	200–300	10,925
Two contemporary rectangular trays	200–300	10,925
Portrait of a President, by William Manchester, inscribed by the author, "For Jacqueline Bouvier Kennedy with admiration and respect . . ."	400–600	11,327
*Pair of English enamel candlesticks	900–1,200	11,500
*Pair of English enamel candlesticks	600–800	11,500
Embossed and watercolor bird picture	1,200–1,800	11,500
Three Studies of Horses, after Edgar Degas	100–150	11,500
Chinese gilt-decorated black-lacquer tilt-top table	2,000–2,500	11,500
Set of ten small earthenware dessert plates	150–250	11,500
Bronze-mounted marble candelabra, mounted as a lamp	1,000–1,500	11,500
Norman Mailer, *Harlot's Ghost*, inscribed "Jackie, I don't know if you will care to read this or not, but I want you to have it. With respect, Norman. Sept.9, '91"	300–500	11,500
Madame Chiang Kai-Shek, *Selected Speeches, 1958–1959*, presentation from the First Lady of China, inscribed, "Mrs. Jacqueline Kennedy . . . December 1964"	600–800	11,500
Fred G. Barnes, *Forty-Minute Plays from Shakespeare*, with pencil notes from Jackie figuring her grades	600–800	11,500
Set of six etchings, *Exotic Figures on Horseback*	1,500–2,000	11,500
*Set of two hand-colored engravings of French interiors and window drapery	100–125	11,500
19th-century Continental school, set of four ink and watercolor drawings	2,000–3,000	11,500
*Charles Parrocel (1688–1752), *Hunters and Their Dogs in a Landscape*	1,000–1,500	11,500
George Chinnery, R.H.A. (1774–1854), *An Overgrown Tomb at Dusk*	3,000–4,000	11,500
Pair of French painted candelabra	600–800	11,500
Chinese small painted leather trunk	350–500	11,500
Louis XVI-style red leather couch	8,000–12,000	11,500
Continental fruitwood hanging shelf	800–1,200	11,500
Carved jade pendant	200–300	11,500
Gold, cultured pearl, ruby, and sapphire pendant ear clips	1,000–1,500	11,500
Five pairs of gilt-metal hoop ear clips	300–400	11,500
Black and gray bead choker	100–150	11,500
Swiss gold and enamel cup	2,500–3,500	11,500
Two matching French silver-gilt beakers	250–450	11,500
Silver waiter with initials "JLB"	75–150	11,500
Silver Old English pattern soup ladle with initial "H"	500–600	11,500
18th-century Bundi school, *Baz Bahadur and Rupmati Hunting in a Landscape*	2,500–3,500	11,500
Delhi school, *The Mughal Emperor Aurangzeb as a Prince Spearing Raging Elephant Before His Father, Shah Jahan*	700–1,000	11,500
James Seymour, *A Canter Along the Wall of a Riding House*	4,000–6,000	11,500
John James Audubon, *Arctic Tern*	3,000–5,000	11,500
American school, *Still Life*, watercolor on linen,	300–500	11,500
Two Nikon 35-mm cameras and four additional lenses	300–500	11,500
Rangefinder camera	200–300	11,500
John F. Kennedy, group of twenty-three volumes	500–700	11,500
John F. Kennedy, group of eight works, one book and ten albums	300–500	11,500
Painted metal blackamoor figure and green-painted basket planter	50–100	11,500
Two Irish woolwork pictures	300–400	11,500
Three Japanese porcelain blue and white saucers	300–500	11,500
Charles Sarka (1879–1960), *Boy in a Landscape*	300–500	11,500
White House guides, group of various editions	300–500	11,500
White House guides, group of various editions	300–500	11,500
Korean dragon jar mounted as a lamp	3,000–,5,000	11,500
Victorian child's puzzle of sailing ship	700–900	11,500
Large brass cigar box monogrammed "ASO"	200–300	11,500
Photograph of an Aaron Shikler portrait	50–75	11,500
Victorian silver paper knife	300–400	12,075
Chinese export porcelain oval dish	200–300	12,650
*Pair of English enamel candlesticks	600–800	12,650
Silver chalice, Cartier	100–150	12,650

Item	Estimate	Price
*Jardinière	100–150	12,650
19th-century black-lacquered papier-mâché and wood worktable	600–800	12,650
Woman in Sedan Chair Attended by Two Men in Blue Coats, pen and ink with watercolor	2,000–3,000	12,650
Blue and white Chinese porcelain garden seats	1,500–2,500	12,650
Japanese porcelain mouse on a corncob	700–1,000	12,650
English electroplate cakestand	80–120	12,650
19th-century gilt-decorated black tray	100–150	12,650
Group of four volumes about Winston S. Churchill	300–500	12,650
The White House: An Historic Guide, Mrs. Kennedy's copy of the official White House guidebook	700–1,000	12,650
19th-century Continental school, set of eight watercolors, interiors with figures and a landscape	3,000–4,000	12,650
19th-century Chinese school, *Napoleon's Residence, The Site of Napoleon's Tomb,* and *Napoleon on His Deathbed,* three watercolors	1,000–1,500	12,650
Isidore Alexandre Augustin Pils (1813–1875), *Fontainebleau*	1,200–1,800	12,650
19th-century Continental school, *An Arab Horseman with Rifle*	600–800	12,650
*Pair of Coalport porcelain oval dishes	500–700	12,650
Louis XVI-style beige-upholstered chair	600–800	12,650
Group of gold ear clips, various designs	1,000–1,200	12,650
18-karat gold, colored stone, and seed pearl ear clips	1,000–1,500	12,650
Bangle bracelets	200–300	12,650
Two pairs of gilt-metal earrings	150–250	12,650
Two gilt-metal chain belts	300–400	12,650
Pair of gilt-metal earclips and gilt-metal chain necklace	300–400	12,650
Two pairs of silvered-metal ear clips	200–300	12,650
Pair of simulated turquoise, amethyst, and diamond dress clips	300–400	12,650
Two pairs of simulated diamond and colored stone ear clips	300–400	12,650
Silver trophy cup	650–850	12,650
Indian polychrome wood figure of a maharaja	1,000–1,500	12,650
716–30 B.C. Egyptian bronze figure of Osiris	200–300	12,650
Group of five pieces of ethnographic jewelry in leather trunk	1,000–1,500	12,650
Oliver Smith, *Decor Design for "The Embassy" in "My Fair Lady,"* watercolor	1,000–1,500	12,650
Indian art, group of nine volumes	600–900	12,650
Armand Hammer, *The Quest of the Romanoff Treasure*, inscribed by the author to President and Mrs. Kennedy	500–700	12,650
Jacqueline Onassis, *The Bouvier Years*, group of four books	400–600	12,650
Daniel Maclise, *Study of a Leopard*	500–600	12,650
Maple folding table	250–350	12,650
20th-century British school, *A Bay Horse with P. Edgley Up*	600–800	12,650
19th-century American school, *Ship on Rough Seas*, watercolor	150–300	12,650
Letter from Thomas Jefferson, with presentation from Pierre Salinger	300–500	12,650
The White House, group of seventeen volumes	600–800	12,650
Kennedy presidency, group of seven volumes, inscribed to Mrs. Kennedy	500–700	12,650
Paul B. Fay, Jr., *The Pleasure of His Company*	500–700	12,650
White House and presidency, group of fifty volumes	300–500	12,650
The Times History of the War, twenty-two volumes	800–1,200	12,650
Periodicals, approximately 250, containing photos and articles of Mrs. Kennedy and her family	100–200	12,650
American history, group of four volumes	800–1,200	12,650
Isabella I, Queen of Spain, signed document, 5 August 1500	1,000–1,500	12,650
Biography, group of nine volumes	800–1,200	12,650
*Pair of cream-colored earthenware orange tubs	60–90	12,650
Kuniyasu, *Portrait of a Courtesan and Attendant*	150–250	12,650
J. Wood, *The White Window*, oil on wood	600–800	12,650
Robert Stackhouse, "*Sailings*" at the Hudson River Museum, Oak and Cedar	3,000–4,000	12,650
Leonor Fini, *Portrait of a Woman*, India ink on paper	300–500	12,650
Eliot Porter, *In Wilderness is the Preservation of the World*	700–1,000	12,650
Set of twenty-eight Chinese octagonal plates	2,500–3,000	12,650
Japanese Imari scalloped bowl	75–125	12,650
Louis XV-style candlestick mounted as a lamp	400–600	12,650
19th-century black papier-mâché tray	100–150	12,650
Painted oval tray-top occasional table	200–300	12,650
Photograph of an Aaron Shikler portrait	50–75	12,650
Studio of Jean-Antoine Watteau, *Three Studies of a Cat*	1,000–1,500	13,225
Indian art, group of fifteen volumes	400–600	13,225
19th-century American school, *The Yellow Horse*	600–800	13,225
Watercolor study of an ostrich	3,000–5,000	13,225
*19th-century French school oil painting, *A Park View*	800–1,200	13,800
The Presidents of the United States 1789–1962: A Selected List of References	1,000–1,500	13,800
Federico Zuccaro (1540–1609), *Half-Length Portrait of a Man with White Ruff and Cloak*	6,000–8,000	13,800
Studio of Jean Berain (1640–1711), *Design for a Ballet Costume*	3,000–5,000	13,800
18th-century fruitwood commode	6,000–8,000	13,800
18-karat gold brooch, young girl with headdress	150–300	13,800
Group of four wristwatches, Timex, Pulsar, and Swiss Army	400–500	13,800
Gilt-metal cuff bracelet and bangle bracelet	150–200	13,800
Sterling silver St. Christopher medal	150–200	13,800

Item	Estimate	Price
Group of metal bangle bracelets	150–200	13,800
Simulated hematite bead necklace	150–250	13,800
French gold-mounted agate snuff box, circa 1743	4,000–6,000	13,800
George III silver dinner plate, 1732	500–700	13,800
Ballet, pair of illustrated volumes	200–300	13,800
Reverse painting on glass, depicting a military figure on horseback	200–400	13,800
19th-century American school, *House By a Lake*	100–200	13,800
Photo facsimile of deed of Virginia land, gift from LBJ, Dec. 1963	200–300	13,800
John F. Kennedy memorials, group of twenty-one volumes	400–600	13,800
Harvard Class of 1940: 25th Anniversary Report	800–1,200	13,800
Chinese porcelain milk jug, circa 1780	100–150	13,800
Greek icon of the Deesis, 18th century	900–1,200	13,800
Richard Garnett, *The International Library of Famous Literature*	1,000–1,500	13,800
*Chippendale-style white painted chest of drawers	600–800	13,800
Two wooden wall mirrors	100–150	13,800
William Walton, *A Political Rally*	800–1,200	13,800
Aaron Shikler, *A Study of Caroline Kennedy Standing*	1,500–2,500	13,800
Paul Louis de Giafferi, *L'Histoire du costume féminin français*, inscribed "Jacqueline Bouvier Kennedy, given to me by Uncle Hugh, March 17, 1963, Book I Always Loved at Merrywood"	600–800	13,800
Raymond Crosby, *Three Women*, pencil on paper	500–700	13,900
French porcelain inkwell and cover	150–250	14,375
Two gilt-metal pendants and a belt buckle	250–350	14,375
Photograph of an Aaron Shikler portrait	50–75	14,375
Set of eleven Ashworth ironstone pudding plates	700–1,000	14,950
19th-century gilt-decorated black kneehole dressing table	1,800–2,200	14,950
Electroplate flatware set (incomplete) engraved with the intitial "K"	100–200	14,950
Eldon Dedini cartoon, "I don't know, lately, *everything* looks like Jackie Kennedy to me"	300–500	14,950
17th-century Flemish school, *Study of a Dog*	7,000–9,000	14,950
*Odilon Redon, *Study of Trees*	3,000–5,000	14,950
Augustus Edwin John (1878–1961), *Portrait of William Butler Yeats*	10,000–15,000	14,950
*19th-century French tapestry-covered pillows	150–250	14,950
Pair of ormolu Japanese porcelain and marble candlesticks	7,000–9,000	14,950
Pair of Louis XVI white and gray tabourets	3,000–4,000	14,950
Walnut table *vide poche*, circa 1800	1,200–1,800	14,950
Chanel, gilt-metal station necklace	300–400	14,950
Group of ivory and ebony jewelry	500–700	14,950
Group of three necklaces, including onyx beads	400–600	14,950
Four cross pendants	400–500	14,950
Sterling silver pen and silver cigarette holder	75–100	14,950
Gold-mounted bloodstone bonbonnière	2,000–3,000	14,950
German enamel snuff box, circa 1765	700–900	14,950
Silver trophy bowl	250–500	14,950
Indian enameled gold box	2,000–3,000	14,950
19th century, eight reverse glass paintings	3,000–5,000	14,950
Oliver Smith, *Decor Design for "Sleeping Beauty,"* Watercolor	1,000–1,500	14,950
John James Audubon, *The Violet Green Cormorant and Townsend's Cormorant*	1,800–2,400	14,950
JFK's copy of the Federal Constitution	800–1,200	14,950
Set of six Doccia porcelain plates, circa 1770	200–300	14,950
Austrian painted vase in the form of a costumed figure	600–800	14,950
Bed-step pot cupboard	400–600	14,950
Enamel miniature of the Holy Virgin, 19th century	300–500	14,950
Mary Faulconer, *Olive Oil*	400–600	14,950
Group of eighty volumes with contributions or edited by Jackie	600–900	14,950
Joseph R. Spiers, *Tom Kitten*, silver print	50–75	14,950
Photograph of an Aaron Shikler portrait	50–75	14,950
*Set of six Louis XVI chairs	2,500–3,500	16,100
*Pencil on paper sketch, *Miss Lane's Reception at the White House*	1,000–1,500	16,100
Staffordshire teapot	500–700	16,100
Lenox porcelain dessert plate from dinner service made for Franklin Delano Roosevelt	400–600	16,100
Italian silver cigarette box inscribed to Jackie	400–600	16,100
*Set of two hand-colored engravings of French interiors and window drapery	100–125	16,100
*17th-century French school, *Study of a Young Man in an Elaborate Costume*	2,500–3,500	16,100
18th-century British school, *Study of a Greyhound*	800–1,200	16,100
*Pair of porcelain jardinières, circa 1810	600–900	16,100
Italian neoclassical parcel-gilt chair	5,000–7,000	16,100
Louis XV-style giltwood mirror	4,000–6,000	16,100
Louis XVI leather-upholstered banquette	6,000–8,000	16,100
Cambodian style suite of gold jewelry, including a necklace, bracelet, and brooch	1,500–2,500	16,100
Gilt-metal filigree and simulated pearl and stone necklace	600–800	16,100
Two pairs of simulated diamond and colored stone ear clips	300–400	16,100
*Three patchwork pillows	400–600	16,100
3rd-century Roman bronze figure of a horse	1,500–2,500	16,100
1st-century Roman Bronze handle	2,000–3,000	16,100
Indian art, group of fourteen volumes	500–700	16,100
Charles Parrocel, *Study of a Soldier on Horseback and Another on Foot*	2,000–3,000	16,100
G. B. Foggini, *Horse Seen from the Rear*	3,000–4,000	16,100
American school, *View on the Hudson Toward Bear Mountain, with a Paddlewheeler at the Center*, oil on canvas	300–500	16,100
Group of colorless glass table glassware	350–500	16,100
19th-century set of caned bedside steps	400–600	16,100
Set of two hand-colored lithographs of French mantelpiece and canopied bed	100–200	16,675
19th-century slipper chair with mother-of-pearl inlay	700–900	17,250
Set of twelve gold-ground pottery plates	300–500	17,250
Set of four hand-colored engravings of exotic costume designs, 18th century	800–1,200	17,250
19th-century French school, *Two Architectural Studies*	4,000–6,000	17,250
Sèvres porcelain, circa 1760, set of seventeen dinner plates	2,500–3,500	17,250
*Pair of Louis XVI white marble candlesticks	200–400	17,250
*Pair of Régence style brass candlesticks	400–600	17,250
Group of miscellaneous gold jewelry, including bangle bracelet, gold pen, arrow-head brooch, and others	750–1000	17,250
Enamel, diamond, and simulated pearl tiger's-head bracelet	500–600	17,250
Gold and enamel cross pendant, Russian	300–400	17,250
Pair of crystal fox cufflinks	300–400	17,250
Group of eleven unmounted round diamonds	500–700	17,250
Simulated black pearl and gold bead multistrand necklace and simulated pearl earclips	150–250	17,250
Pair of simulated diamond cluster ear clips and flower brooch	400–500	17,250
Vermeil and pale green stone necklace and matching ear clips	600–800	17,250
Brown-lacquered Parsons-style coffee table	200–300	17,250
Peggy Burrows, *The First Family*, tempera on board	200–300	17,250
1st/2nd century B.C. Hellenistic marble head of a goddess	2,000–3,000	17,250
3rd-century B.C. Greek terra-cotta figure of a youth	2,000–3,000	17,250
John F. Kennedy, *As We Remember Joe*	1,000–1,500	17,250
John F. Kennedy Memorial at Runnymeade: Dedicatory Remarks, bound and printed for Mrs. Kennedy	400–600	17,250
Group of four portraits and one photograph	300–400	17,250
Marcel Vertes, *Woman in Bikini with Bicycle*	800–1,200	17,250
Pictures of Horses and English Life, by A. J. Munnings, inscribed by Jacqueline Kennedy, "Jacqueline Bouvier Kennedy given to me by Uncle Hugh, March 27 1963 because I loved it growing up at Merrywood"	1,500–2,500	17,250
Young Man in a Gallery, Continental school painting	500–700	18,400
Set of three silver salt and pepper shakers engraved with the initial "K"	400–600	18,400
Yellow upholstered settee	500–800	18,400
Silver cigarette box with amethyst lid	250–350	18,400
Autographed note with framed photo of Walt Whitman	1,200–1,800	18,400
Spode china, "Famille-Rose" partial dinner service	2,500–3,000	18,400
19th-century bronze and ormolu chenets	1,500–2,500	18,400
18th-century tortoiseshell box	3,000–5,000	18,400
Louis XV-style upholstered chair	2,000–3,000	18,400
Gold, enamel, and diamond pendant, Indian	400–600	18,400
Suite of gilt-metal bead and simulated diamond jewelry	500–700	18,400
Silver belt	400–600	18,400
Silver cross necklace	400–600	18,400
Simulated diamond and crystal necklace and two pairs of matching earrings	500–600	18,400
Silver trophy cup	1,200–1,500	18,400
2nd-century Roman marble triple-headed Hekate	3,000–5,000	18,400
1st-century Roman bronze figure of Hygeia	6,000–9,000	18,400
*Victorian needlepoint picture, *A Parrot on a Fruit Branch*	300–500	18,400
John F. Kennedy, *Profiles in Courage*, memorial edition	400–600	18,400
Viennese gold, enamel, and glass cup	1,500–2,000	18,400
Bernard Buffet, *Tête de hibon*, drypoint	500–700	18,400
Etiquette and style, group of five volumes	400–600	18,400
American Federal giltwood wall mirror	200–400	18,400
Oil on canvas, *Full-Length Painting of a Girl in a Fencing Outfit*	200–300	18,400
Silver-plated beaker, engraved, "JK"	100–150	19,550
18th-century Louis XV ebonized table	5,000–7,000	19,550
19th-century Continental school, set of five ink and watercolor drawings	2,000–3,000	19,550
*Jean Baptiste Oudry (1686–1735), *Study of a Hound Baying*	7,000–9,000	19,550
19th-century Turkish school, *Women of the Harem*	1,000–1,500	19,550
19th-century pair of carved ivory urns	3,000–4,000	19,550
*Paris-style porcelain vase, mounted as a lamp	250–350	19,550
Pair of Louis XVI-style cane-backed painted chairs	1,500–2,000	19,550
Two gilt-metal necklaces	300–400	19,550
Gold coin necklace	1,200–1,500	19,550
Group of three bead necklaces	300–400	19,550
Simulated diamond brooch and bangle bracelet	400–600	19,550

Item	Estimate	Price
Group of gilt-metal and simulated diamond jewelry	400–500	19,550
Two pairs of simulated diamond and colored stone ear clips	300–400	19,550
Silver trophy cup	1,500–2,000	19,550
Electroplate dressing table mirror	400–600	19,550
Architectural study of Red Fort of Delhi	2,500–3,500	19,550
Two illustrations from the Victoria and Albert Museum, *Akbarnama*	15,000–20,000	19,550
Illustration from the *Akbarnama*	15,000–20,000	19,550
Peter Tillemans (1684–1734), *A Jockey Standing with a Bay Horse*	1,200–1,800	19,550
Keith Daniel, *Bath Houses*	1,500–2,500	19,550
French school 19th/20th-century, *Cambodian Dancer*, watercolor	200–300	19,550
Uruguay, Ministry of Industry and Work, *Conferencia Interamericana Economica y Social*, inscribed to the president	500–700	19,550
Group of silver-plated pieces, including bucket, tray, ashtray, ice tongs, ice pick, bottle opener, and coasters	200–300	20,700
A. D., 19th/20th-century French school, *Still Life with Flowers*	500–700	20,700
*Louis XVI-style mahogany table *vide poche**	1,500–2,000	20,700
18-karat gold bracelet and gold and diamond brooch	700–900	20,700
18-karat gold chain necklace with ivory cylinders	750–1,000	20,700
Middle Eastern gold belt with emerald and diamonds	2,000–3,000	20,700
Pair of gilt-metal and simulated emerald ear clips and two green glass bead necklaces	300–400	20,700
Four tribal-style necklaces	350–450	20,700
Simulated black pearl necklace and ear clips	400–500	20,700
Guler school, *A Lady on a Terrace Feeding a Parakeet*	7,000–10,000	20,700
Dutch school, *A Gray Stallion in a Landscape*	800–1,200	20,700
Anonymous, *Fish Specimens*	500–600	20,700
Junius Stearns (1810–1885), *Disbrow Cottage in Mamaroneck*	1,500–2,000	20,700
Y. C. Wang, *Lion and Polar Bear*	300–400	20,700
*Berlin porcelain tea and coffee service	600–900	20,700
Pair of French silver wine coasters	1,000–1,500	21,850
*Aert Schouman (1710–1792), *Study of a White Monkey*	2,000–3,000	21,850
Louis XVI-style mahogany bureau plat	700–900	21,850
Gold and amber worry beads	200–300	21,850
Black bead necklace and pair of simulated diamond ear clips	300–400	21,850
Silver ash tray inscribed "N.G.A. 6.8.57 J.B.K."	150–200	21,850
*19th-century British school, *Trumpet Honeysuckle*	600–800	21,850
Kenneth O'Donnell and David Powers, *Johnny, We Hardly Knew Ye*	600–800	21,850
Cape Cod and summer pastimes, group of thirteen volumes	200–300	21,850
Brass-studded leather-covered storage trunk	600–800	21,850
*French painted screen	3,000–5,000	23,000
Coalport porcelain, "Peacock" pattern part dinner service	4,000–6,000	23,000
Electroplate cigarette lighter	800–1,200	23,000
Victorian maple cane-back rocking chair	300–400	23,000
Silver-plated cocktail shaker monogrammed "JBK"	100–200	23,000
*Aert Schouman (1710–1792), *Two Ornamental Fowl with Black Plumage and White Crests in a Landscape*	5,000–7,000	23,000
Canton porcelain, "Famille-Rose" mid-19th-century partial dinner service	9,000–12,000	23,000
Pair of Flemish ivory oval reliefs	3,000–5,000	23,000
Italian neoclassical fruitwood table	2,500–3,500	23,000
Pair of Louis XV floral upholstered chairs	2,000–3,000	23,000
Pair of gold ear clips, designed as Chinese masks	600–800	23,000
Pair of 18-karat gold and green enamel ear clips	2,000–3,000	23,000
14-karat gold and jade brooch	1,000–1,500	23,000
Gold, enamel, and diamond elephant-head bangle bracelet	3,000–5,000	23,000
Simulated seed pearl and diamond bracelet and simulated diamond and stone ear clips	300–400	23,000
Guler school, *A Ruler and His Mistress Strolling by a Pool in a Garden Enclosure*	20,000–30,000	23,000
Charles Baskerville, *Guardians of the Portal of the Temple, Rajasthan, India*	800–1,200	23,000
*Camilla Gandolfi, *Owl on a Rock*, pen and ink drawing	500–700	23,000
Adlai Stevenson, *Looking Outward: Years of Crisis at the United Nations*	1,500–2,000	23,000
*Two hand-colored etchings, circa 1825	100–150	23,000
*Three-paneled canvas screen	200–300	23,000
*French Provincial-style chest of drawers	500–700	23,000
Three decorative prints of JFK	200–300	23,000
Aaron Shikler, *A Portrait Study of Caroline Kennedy*	1,500–2,500	23,000
Victorian black papier-mâché tray	2,000–3,000	24,150
Dean Acheson, *Power and Diplomacy*, with annotations by JFK	5,000–7,000	24,150
19th-century Neopolitan school, pair of watercolors, *View of Mount Vesuvius* and *A View of Naples*	7,000–9,000	24,150
John Ruskin (1819–1900), *The Spanish Steps*	15,000–20,000	24,150
*Pair of Louis XVI ormolu cassollettes	2,500–3,500	24,150
Louis XV painted gilt mirror	1,500–2,500	24,150
18th-century pair of Régence chaises	8,000–12,000	24,150
*Louis XVI gray-painted writing table	1,000–1,500	24,150
Chinese red-lacquered side table	7,500–10,000	24,150
Simulated ruby and emerald bead and pearl choker necklace	300–400	24,150
Simulated pearl necklace and two pairs of simulated pearl and diamond ear clips	150–250	24,150
Coin necklace and coin pendant necklace	150–250	24,150
Jacqueline Bouvier Kennedy, *Botticelli Judith*, watercolor	200–300	24,150
3rd-century B.C. Greek terra-cotta figure of a woman	6,000–9,000	24,150
Antonio Canaletto, *Prospectus Magni Canalis Venetiarum*	2,000–3,000	24,150
Painted leather screen with fox-hunting scene	1,500–2,000	24,150
John James Audubon, *Herring Gull*	3,500–4,500	24,150
John F. Kennedy, group of nine works in sixteen stereo albums	600–800	24,150
Scrimshaw sperm whale's tooth, engraved with a portrait of JFK	300–500	24,150
Louis XVI-style malachite tazza	200–300	24,150
Mother-of-pearl-handled magnifying glass and letter opener	200–300	24,150
Aaron Shikler, *A Portrait Study of John F. Kennedy, Jr.*	1,500–2,500	24,150
Four engraved aquatints, *Select Views of India*	4,000–6,000	24,725
*Pair of Italian neoclassical armchairs	1,500–2,000	25,300
English electroplate salver engraved with the initials "JLBK"	50–100	25,300
*Circle of Giovanni Battista Tiepolo, *Study of Three Puchinelli Gathered around a Brazier*	2,000–3,000	25,300
Pairs of shell ear clips	400–600	25,300
Simulated diamond and sapphire ear clips and dress clip	250–350	25,300
John Nost Sartorius (1759–1828), *"Floss," A Saddled Bay Hunter Tied to a Tree in a Landscape*	8,000–12,000	25,300
Encyclopaedia Britannica	500–700	25,300
Viscount d'Abernon, *The 18th Decisive Battle of the World: Warsaw 1920*	1,000–1,500	25,300
*Pericle Fazzini (Italian, 1913–87), *Buttero (Horse and Rider)*, bronze sculpture	1,500–2,500	25,300
Twenty-nine lapel pins representing various countries visited or entertained by the Kennedys	400–600	25,300
Three cushions, two striped silk, one floral	50–100	25,300
Pen and ink, *Birdcage*, with watercolor, *Basket of Cherries*	100–150	25,300
Malthe M. Hasselriis, *Two Portrait Miniatures of John F. Kennedy*	200–400	25,300
Aaron Shikler, *A Portrait Study of Caroline Kennedy*	1,500–2,500	25,300
22-karat gold collar	1,000–1,200	25,875
Gold and garnet hinged bracelet	1,000–1,200	25,875
Late 19th-century gold, diamond, and enamel pendant	750–1,000	25,875
Diamond bird brooch	2,000–3,000	25,875
Simulated colored stone bib necklace	400–500	25,876
Two gold pendants and a gilt metal charm bracelet	200–300	26,450
18-karat gold diamond and green glass pendant, in the shape of Martha's Vineyard	3,000–4,000	26,450
Silver, gold, and enamel crucifix pendant	600–800	26,450
History and travel, group of thirteen volumes	600–900	26,450
John Austin, *Tuckernuck Landscape, Nantucket, Massachusetts*	100–200	26,450
Upholstered club chair with floral chintz slipcover	200–250	27,600
Silver plate inscribed "To Jacqueline and John . . . from the Governor of Rhode Island"	200–300	27,600
Oil on board, 18th/19th century, *A Gathering of Birds in an Extensive Landscape*	10,000–15,000	27,600
19th-century Bessarabian kilim rug	2,000–3,000	27,600
Two silk rope and simulated stone necklaces	500–600	27,600
Two pairs of gilt metal and simulated diamond ear clips	200–300	27,600
Silver-gilt belt, Cartier	500–700	27,600
Four silver ashtrays with initial "K"	400–600	27,600
*Set of four gilt-decorated églomisé pictures	1,800–2,400	27,600
Aaron Shikler, *John F. Kennedy, Jr., Seated*	2,000–3,00	27,600
Aaron Shikler, *Vase of Flowers with One White Rose*	750–1,000	27,600
English silver compote engraved "JLB"	700–1,000	28,750
Louis XVI kingwood and tulipwood table	800–1,200	28,750
Set of four Louis XVI gray and blue chairs	4,000–6,000	28,750
Biedermeier walnut and fruitwood etagère	6,000–8,000	28,750
Pair of 18-karat gold and diamond ear clips, designed as knots	1,500–2,000	28,750
Pair of gold and sapphire antelope-head bangle bracelets	2,000–3,000	28,750
Gold and cultured pearl pendant brooch	1,500–2,000	28,750
Gold pendant earrings, designed as flower-filled urns	800–1,200	28,750
Simulated pearl and diamond bead necklace and matching ear clips	400–500	28,750
Lilly Cushing, *Portrait of Jacqueline Kennedy Onassis*	150–200	28,750
Silver-gilt and cut-glass dresser set	1,800–2,200	28,750
Swiss "Golf-sport" stroke counter	50–100	28,750
Marble replica of the head of Hermes	4,000–6,000	28,750
Namingha, *Mask*, oil on canvas	1,000–1,500	28,750
Ireland and the Irish, group of ten volumes	300–500	28,750
Louis XVI-style three-light bouillotte lamp	1,200–1,800	28,750
Contemporary wallpaper screen	3,000–5,000	29,900
*Ravault hand-colored engraving, c. 1840, after Isabey and Percier	150–250	29,900
*English school, circa 1800, *Caricatures of Men and Women: A Set of Ten*	3,000–5,000	29,900
19th-century mahogany bedside cupboard	1,500–2,000	29,900
Two gold brooches	600–800	29,900
Gold and hardstone worry beads	400–600	29,900

Item	Estimate	Price
Pair of yellow metal gypsy bangle bracelets	300–500	29,900
Heart-shaped silver candy dish	150–200	29,900
Madeline Hewes, *Catfish Creek*	300–500	29,900
Clifton Tomson, *Two Bays and a Grey in a Landscape*	5,000–7,000	29,900
Seven hand-colored engravings of ornithological subjects	1,200–1,600	29,900
John Austin, *Close Up of Brandt Point Light, Nantucket, Massachusetts*	150–250	29,900
R. B. Sprague, *A Church with Three Crosses*, oil on canvas	800–1,200	29,900
Berlin porcelain reticulated bowl	400–600	29,900
*Watercolor painting of snow owl	2,000–3,000	31,050
*Paris porcelain vases, mounted as lamps	1,500–2,000	31,050
Watercolor, *Jackie and Lee on a Camel*	500–700	31,050
Adlai Stevenson, *What I Think*	2,000–3,000	31,050
Ruby, diamond, and ivory crucifix pendant	200–300	31,050
The White House Gallery of Official Portraits of the Presidents	400–600	31,050
Belleek porcelain "Shamrock Ware" tea and coffee service	600–900	31,050
Stetson brown leather hatbox with tag stating, "The President"	200–300	31,625
Two gold commemorative coins; one from launching of USS *John F. Kennedy*, another with a ship and Hebrew inscription	150–200	31,625
Diamond bar brooch	2,000–3,000	31,625
Group of gold animal-head jewelry, including rings and ear clips	1,200–1,500	31,625
22-karat gold lion's-head collar	750–1,000	31,625
22-karat gold flower brooch	1,000–1,200	31,625
Emerald, ruby, and cultured pearl brooch	3,000–4,000	31,625
*Chinese porcelain potpourri jar and cover	250–350	31,625
Upholstered settee with cream slipcover and two floral pillows	1,000–1,500	32,200
George B. Tatum, *Penn's Great Town: 250 Years of Philadelphia Architecture*	400–600	32,200
Louis XVI mahogany secretaire	7,000–9,000	32,200
18th-century Thai gold jar	3,000–4,000	32,200
Albert York, *Pink Daisies in a Glass Jar*, oil on panel	1,500–2,500	32,200
*Mahogany footstool	100–150	33,350
Pair of silver candelabra, Tiffany and Co., engraved "JBK"	500–700	33,350
Garnet and diamond ring	1,200–1,500	33,350
*Carzou, *Garden Gates Surrounded by Trees*	800–1,200	33,350
Bound copy, *Inauguration of the British Memorial to John F. Kennedy*	1,500–2,500	34,500
Set of twelve white metal table mats engraved with the initials "JJK"	600–800	34,500
Memorial Addresses in the Congress of the United States and Tributes in Eulogy of John Fitzgerald Kennedy, Late a President of the United States	3,000–5,000	34,500
18-karat gold chain necklace	600–800	34,500
Pair of red tourmaline and amethyst pendant ear clips	800–1,200	34,500
Miniature oval pendant	800–1,200	34,500
Gold key pendant engraved "109"	200–300	34,500
Four cross pendants	400–500	34,500
Victorian-style silver pitcher	1,500–2,500	34,500
Kangra school, *A Lady Enticing a Peacock with a Strand of Pearls*	15,000–20,000	34,500
3rd-century Roman marble head of a man	7,000–10,000	34,500
Leather hunting saddle, Boston	300–500	34,500
Three leather head covers with initials "JFK"	100–150	34,500
Padraic Colum, *A Treasury of Irish Folklore*, with note, "In JFK's Bedroom in the White House, JBK, 1964"	1,500–2,500	34,500
Aaron Shikler, *John F. Kennedy, Jr., Reading*	3,500–5,000	34,500
4th-century B.C. Greek terra-cotta figure of Aphrodite	4,000–6,000	35,650
William Higgins, *Study of a Leopard*	1,800–2,500	35,650
Aaron Shikler, portrait study, *Caroline Kennedy Seated*	2,500–3,500	36,800
Thirteen volumes about ballet	600–800	36,800
Albert York, *Geranium in a Blue Pot with Fallen Leaf and Bird*, oil on Wood	3,000–5,000	36,800
French school, 20th century, *Open Car Welcoming Parade, France*	800–1,200	36,800
19th-century Empire ormolu and cut-glass chandelier	25,000–35,000	37,375
*Louis XVI mahogany console desserte	8,000–12,000	37,375
Group of four gold rings of various designs, sizes 5 through 7 1/2	300–400	37,375
Two gold bangle bracelets	1,000–1,500	37,375
18-karat yellow and white gold heart-shaped ear clips	3,000–4,000	37,375
Pair of diamond and royal blue enamel ear clips	7,500–10,000	37,375
Gold, enamel, and diamond snake bangle-bracelet	5,000–7,000	37,375
Set of five Lourioux porcelain pots de crème with stand	100–150	37,375
*Wedgwood creamware dinner service	3,500–5,000	37,375
J. B., 19th-century Continental school, *Still Life with Pink Roses Resting on a Marble Ledge*	10,000–15,000	37,950
John F. Kennedy, *To Turn the Tide*, signed by the president	1,500–2,500	37,950
Two simulated pearl necklaces and simulated diamond ear clips	400–500	39,100
Color photograph of Earth, taken from *Apollo 10*, signed to Ari Onassis from the crew of *Apollo 10*	500–700	39,100
*Early Victorian dressing table	1,500–2,500	40,250
Silver-gilt dressing table items	300–400	40,250
*Louis XV fruitwood bureau plat table	7,000–9,000	40,250
Pair of silver candelabra	1,000–1,500	40,250
Fourteen volumes about music, some inscribed to President and Mrs. Kennedy	400–600	40,250
Cartier lady's gold wristwatch	1,500–2,000	40,250
Moroccan gold belt with emerald and diamonds	4,000–6,000	40,250
Gilt metal cross brooch and pendant cross necklace	200–300	40,250
2360–2195 B.C. Egyptian banded alabaster jar	6,000–9,000	40,250
Charles Baskerville, *Tiger*	500–700	40,250
Circle of John Wootton, *A Bay Horse in a Landscape with Groom, Said to Be "Flying Childers"*	30,000–40,000	40,250
Encyclopaedia Britannica World Atlas	400–600	40,250
Framed *Ms. Magazine* cover featuring Jackie and Gloria Steinem, signed by Ms. Steinem and magazine staffers	400–600	40,250
Group of four prints	150–200	40,250
Robert Berk, *John F. Kennedy: A Portrait Bust*	500–1,000	40,250
Photograph of JFK, mounted, framed, and signed by the academics of his administration	800–1,200	40,250
*Creamware candlesticks	250–350	40,250
Aaron Shikler, *Study of Jacqueline Kennedy, Seated*	8,000–12,000	40,250
Marble torso of Aphrodite	6,000–9,000	41,400
Albert York, *A Purple Anemone with Zinnias in a Glass Jar*, oil on canvas	2,000–4,000	41,400
*Radloff, *Fragment of Eden (End of Summer)*, tempera on board	400–600	41,400
Photograph of an Aaron Shikler portrait	50–75	41,400
*German earthenware tub	800–1,200	42,550
A Complete Treatise on the Conjugation of French Verbs, inscribed on front cover, "Jacqueline Bouvier, Form 2, Tel–Woodley 4020"	500–800	42,550
Simulated turquoise, diamond, and ruby necklace, bracelet, and brooch set	500–700	42,550
Set of twelve silver ashtrays with initials "JBK"	150–200	42,550
Watercolor study of milky stork	20,000–30,000	43,125
*19th-century rosewood games table	3,500–4,500	43,125
*18th-century brass-mounted mahogany console desserte, with marble top	8,000–12,000	43,125
*Fruitwood and sycamore parquetry table *vide poche*	10,000–15,000	43,125
*19th-century Victorian needlepoint rug	6,000–8,000	43,125
18-karat gold wristwatch, Uri, France	1,000–1,500	43,125
Gold, enamel, and diamond cameo bracelet	5,000–7,000	43,125
Pair of diamond chandelier earrings	3,000–4,000	43,125
Gold, ruby, and diamond pillbox	3,000–4,000	43,125
19th-century Thai gold spice box and cover	400–600	43,125
Oliver Smith, *Decor Design for Camelot*, pencil on board	1,000–1,500	43,125
*After Sir Edwin Henry Landseer, *The Cavalier's Pets*	700–900	43,125
Jamie Wyeth, lithograph, *John F. Kennedy*	400–600	43,700
Pair of palm tree candlesticks, Tiffany and Co.	1,200–1,800	43,700
*Madeline Hewes, *Arab in Desert Seated on Carpet with Tiger*	300–400	43,700
Set of twenty-two French glass tumblers	300–500	43,700
18th-century bronze mantel clock	5,000–7,000	46,000
Why England Slept, John F. Kennedy	3,000–5,000	46,000
Aaron Shikler, portrait study, *Jacqueline Kennedy Onassis Seated*	7,000–10,000	46,000
Pine and maple long table	1,500–2,500	46,000
19th-century pair of ormolu and bronze candelabra	10,000–15,000	46,000
Pearl and diamond ring	750–1,000	46,000
Leather hunting saddle, Milan	300–500	46,000
A Christmas Picture, watercolor, inscribed "Jacqueline Kennedy, Noel 1961"	200–300	48,300
*Mahogany marble-top pier table	8,000–12,000	48,875
*Louis XV–style lamp	700–900	48,875
Silver-cased Tiffany tape measure	500–700	48,875
Charles X ormolu and bronze mantel clock	4,000–6,000	48,875
*Italian neoclassical games table	5,000–7,000	48,875
Gold rope lion's-head necklace	1,000–1,200	48,875
Simulated turquoise, emerald, and diamond necklace	100–150	48,875
*Austrian silver and enamel table clock	1,000–1,500	48,875
*Oil on Canvas, *A Whippet and a King Charles Spaniel on a Red Cushion*	2,000–4,000	48,875
Painted plastic model of Air Force One	300–500	48,875
Carpet, approx. 18 x 8 feet	2,000–3,000	51,750
Aaron Shikler, portrait study, *Jacqueline Kennedy Onassis Seated*	7,000–10,000	51,750
*Judith Lewis (mid-18th-century), *Elegant Figures Preparing for the Hunt*	20,000–30,000	51,750
Pair of 22-karat gold cuff bangle bracelets	2,000–3,000	51,750
Diamond and enamel butterfly brooch	15,000–20,000	51,750
Elaine de Kooning (1919–1989), *Portrait of John F. Kennedy*	1,500–2,500	51,750
Black-glazed Greek pitcher, 4th century B.C.	20,000–30,000	54,625
Aaron Shikler, *A Study of Caroline and John Kennedy*	2,000–3,000	54,625
*19th-century rococo style fruitwood and mahogany commode	5,000–7,000	57,500
Cartier lady's gold wristwatch	1,500–2,000	57,500
Gold and amethyst bead necklace	1,500–2,000	57,500
*Austrian silver and enamel table clock	1,000–1,500	57,500
2nd-century Roman marble torso of a god or hero	10,000–15,000	57,500
Simulated pearl and diamond ear clips and simulated gray pearl necklace	200–300	57,500
Watercolor study of gray pelican	20,000–30,000	60,250
David Ben-Gurion, *Israel: Years of Challenge*, inscribed, "To Mrs. Jacqueline B. Kennedy with deep admiration. D. Ben-Gurion, Sdeh-Boker, 18.12.63"	1,500–2,500	61,900

Item	Estimate	Price
Painted pine two-drawer table, 19th-century	2,000–3,000	63,000
18th-century Louis XV upholstered chairs	15,000–25,000	63,000
Piaget, 18-karat gold diamond and emerald wristwatch	2,000–3,000	63,000
Fabergé gold, silver, and diamond hair ornament	7,000–9,000	63,000
19th-century Italian marble medallion relief	12,000–18,000	63,000
Robot K–44 putter	200–300	63,000
Elaine de Kooning (1919–1989), *Portrait of John F. Kennedy*	1,500–2,500	63,000
Identification used by JFK and staff on trips	2,000–3,000	63,000
★19th-century maple sewing table	1,500–2,000	63,000
Emerald, ruby, and diamond brooch	5,000–7,000	65,750
MacGregor 147 putter, "The Krook"	200–300	65,750
★Empire-style slant-front desk	1,500–2,000	68,500
Profiles in Courage, memorial edition	3,000–5,000	68,500
Aaron Shikler, portrait study, *Jacqueline Kennedy Onassis Seated*	4,000–6,000	68,500
Nicolas-Louis-Albert Delerive, *Equestrian Portrait, Said to Be Peter the Great*	20,000–30,000	68,500
18-karat gold handbag	2,000–3,000	68,500
Gold charm bracelet, with twenty-five various charms including a slipper, a fish, a padlock, and others	1,500–2,000	68,500
Diamond and enamel miniature brooch	2,000–3,000	68,500
18-karat gold and coral sculpture	8,000–12,000	68,500
Photographs of Aaron Shikler portraits	75–100	68,500
★Pair of horse paintings, oil on canvas	2,000–3,000	74,000
Emerald and diamond pendant, brooch, and chain necklace	10,000–12,000	74,000
John James Audubon, *The Great Blue Heron*	30,000–50,000	74,000
Edward, Duke of Windsor, *A King's Story: The Memoirs of the Duke of Windsor*, inscribed to the president from the author	1,000–1,500	74,000
Simulated pearl necklace and simulated pearl and diamond ear clips	400–600	76,750
Scelles, 18th century, *Equestrian Portrait of a Member of the Herbert de La Pleignière Family*	25,000–35,000	79,500
Johann Georg de Hamilton (1672–1737), *An Equestrian Portrait of a Nobleman*	25,000–35,000	79,500
★18th-century Italian neoclassical table	5,000–7,000	79,500
1992 BMW four-door sedan	18,000–22,000	79,500
Two terra-cotta horses, 3rd century B.C.	12,000–18,000	82,250
★Hide-covered rocking horse	2,000–3,000	85,000
★Victorian mahogany high chair	1,500–2,000	85,000
Domenico Scianteschi, two oil-on-canvas paintings, *Architectural Capriccios with Figures, One Depicting an Episode in the Life of St. Matthew*	60,000–80,000	85,000
★Pair of Louis XVI ormolu black and white marble obelisks	10,000–15,000	85,000
Gold and black enamel lighter with initial "J"	300–400	85,000
Diamond bracelet, approximately 8 carats of diamonds mounted in 18-karat gold	6,000–8,000	85,000
Cabochon emerald and diamond ring	10,000–15,000	85,000
Emerald bead, cabochon ruby, diamond, and pearl ear clips	20,000–30,000	85,000
Simulated pearl necklaces (triple and double strands) and two pairs of gilt-metal ear clips	400–500	85,000
Rene Bouché, *Portrait of Jacqueline Kennedy*	800–1,200	85,000
Pair of Louis XVI red leather chairs	20,000–30,000	90,500
Simulated diamond and colored stone necklace and ear clips	1,000–1,500	90,500
Leather hunting saddle, Switzerland	300–500	90,500
18-karat gold, diamond, and colored stone bracelet	15,000–20,000	96,000
Gold enamel tiger bangle bracelet	6,000–8,000	96,000
Pair of emerald and diamond pendants	15,000–20,000	96,000
Elaine de Kooning, *Portrait of John F. Kennedy*, charcoal on paper	3,000–4,000	101,500
18-karat gold, colored stone, and diamond scarecrow brooch	1,200–1,500	101,500
Gold elephant bangle bracelet	600–800	101,500
Cabochon ruby and diamond ring	4,000–6,000	101,500
Black "stone" bead double strand necklace	200–300	101,500
★Gilded brass and mahogany card table	35,000–45,000	107,000
18-karat gold and ruby moon ear clips	1,000–1,200	112,500
Two simulated pearl necklaces and a pair of simulated diamond and pearl ear clips	250–350	112,500
Marie Laurencin, *Femme au cheval*, oil on canvas	60,000–80,000	112,500
★Charles François Daubigny (1817–1878), *Les Bords de l'Oise*	30,000–50,000	118,000
Louis XV small red Morocco leather casket, circa 1770	25,000–35,000	118,000
Coral and diamond flower brooch and matching ear clips	15,000–20,000	123,500
18-karat gold, carved coral, and diamond horse bracelet	10,000–15,000	123,500
Inaugural Addresses of the Presidents of the United States, inscribed by Jackie to her mother and stepfather	3,000–5,000	123,500
18-karat gold, sapphire, and diamond table clock	7,500–10,00	129,000
★Two Louis XVI upholstered chairs	10,000–15,000	134,500
Norman Rockwell, *Portrait of John F. Kennedy*	8,000–12,000	134,500
President Kennedy's copy, *Inaugural Addresses of the Presidents of the United States*	10,000–15,000	134,500
Aaron Shikler, *Study of Jacqueline Kennedy Standing*	5,000–7,000	134,500
Garnet and diamond flower brooch	12,000–15,000	145,500
John Singer Sargent, *Venetian Girl*, watercolor	80,000–120,000	156,500
Aaron Shikler, *Study for the White House Portrait of Jacqueline Kennedy*, oil on panel	10,000–15,000	156,500
Pear-shaped diamond ring	60,000–70,000	156,500
Ruby, emerald, and diamond bead necklace	60,000–80,000	156,500
Ebonized baby grand piano, Henry F. Miller, Boston	3,000–5,000	167,500
★Martin Drolling (1752–1817), *Portrait of Barthelemy Charles, Comte de Dreux-Nancre, Standing at a Balustrade with a Landscape Beyond*	80,000–120,000	167,500
Gold cuff bangle-bracelets	1,500–2,000	167,500
Aaron Shikler, *Study for the White House Portrait of Jacqueline Kennedy*	8,000–12,000	178,500
Aaron Shikler, *Study for the White House Portrait of Jacqueline Kennedy*	10,000–15,000	184,000
Leather office set, monogrammed "JFK"	1,200–1,500	189,500
Aaron Shikler, *Portrait of Jacqueline Kennedy Seated on a Couch*	8,000–12,000	195,000
Triple-strand simulated pearl necklace	500–700	211,500
John Singer Sargent, *Head of an Arab*, watercolor	100,000–125,000	222,500
Robert Rauschenberg, *Drawing for President of the USA with Dante*	80,000–100,000	244,500
Ruby and diamond necklace	75,000–100,000	250,000
Diamond and emerald drop necklace	1000,000–125,000	277,500
Ruby and diamond ring	20,000–30,000	288,500
Cabochon colored stone and diamond pendant necklace	75,000–100,000	288,500
John Wootton (1683–1764), *Lord Bateman's Arabian*	80,000–120,000	343,500
Pair of cabochon ruby and diamond pendant ear clips	25,000–35,000	360,000
Set of Ben Hogan Power Thrust irons with leather bag	700–900	387,500
Kunzite and diamond ring	6,000–8,000	415,000
★Oak rocking chair	3000–5000	442,500
An oak rocking chair	3,000–5,000	453,500
Walnut humidor	2,000–2,500	574,500
Set of MacGregor woods with golf bag	700–900	772,500
★Louis XVI ormolu-mounted mahogany table	20,000–30,000	1,432,500
Lesotho III 40.42-carat diamond	500,000–600,000	2,587,500
Blue and white Chinese porcelain two-tier box and cover	500–700	withdrawn
Collected Civil War Memorabilia: John Vernon Bouvier	600–800	withdrawn
Sékov Touré, inscribed book	600–800	withdrawn

TAPE MEASURE

ESTIMATE: $500-700

PRICE: $48,875

THIS **T**IFFANY TAPE MEASURE WAS ENGRAVED WITH JACKIE'S INITIALS, JBK. AFTER THE ITEM WAS AUCTIONED, TIFFANY'S WAS FLOODED WITH REQUESTS FOR SILVER TAPE MEASURES.